Retirement: Stop Worrying & Start Planning

Eric Muir

Retirement: Stop Worrying & Start Planning
Copyright ©2016 Eric Muir

ISBN 978-1506-901-38-1 PBK
ISBN 978-1506-901-39-8 HC /Jacket
ISBN 978-1506-901-40-4 HC/Laminate
ISBN 978-1506-901-41-1 EBOOK

LCCN 2016932048

February 2016

Published and Distributed by
First Edition Design Publishing, Inc.
P.O. Box 20217, Sarasota, FL 34276-3217
www.firsteditiondesignpublishing.com

I want to thank my wife, Carol, who has loyally stood by me for the past 33 years and counting.

Additionally, my faith in Jesus Christ is the most fundamental part of my life. I am not perfect. Only He is, but it is His life in me that I celebrate and am thankful for.

I hope this book will assist Canadians in need of financial planning and retirement guidance.

Acknowledgements

This book is based on my experiences as a financial advisor over the past 30 years.

We can all point to people who have influenced our thinking. John Templeton, Warren Buffet and Bill Kanko during his days at AIM Trimark were the primary influences in my approach to managing investments.

I am indebted to accountant Phil Kelly for the value-added information he provided regarding the myriad of tax questions we raised. I am also appreciative of our Raymond James Wealth Management division for providing tax and financial planning advice. I must also acknowledge lawyer Steve Miller. Steve and I have presented estate planning seminars together for the past 20 years.

I would be remiss if I didn't acknowledge my team for their tireless efforts on behalf of our clients. In particular, thanks to my associate Tracey MacDonald for her dedication to looking after our clients and her encouragement in writing this book. I'm also indebted to Sherri McDermott, who hunted down all the various items I requested to finish the book.

The encouragement of a spouse should never be overlooked. In my case, my wife Carol has been a blessing as I have trudged through completing the book.

Lastly, thanks to Mike Dubes for helping edit this book and for spending the time with me over this past year. It won't be forgotten.

Table of Contents

Foreword

Twenty years ago, I began working with Eric Muir, conducting seminars for his clients on retirement, estate planning and other related issues. I've had the pleasure of working with Eric ever since.

Twenty years ago, I also carried a pager so I could be summoned to the hospital for the birth of our first child. A lot of things have changed since then, but the challenges to a fulfilling retirement have remained the same. Eric wisely addresses one of the major challenges — procrastination — in the very first chapter of his excellent book.

Delaying decisions is an easy trap to fall into. As an estate planning lawyer, I interact with a lot of very sophisticated business people who routinely postpone important estate planning issues because "there will be time for that later." I've spoken to people who actually put off creating a will because they fear doing so will hasten their death! For many, not thinking about the issue helps make it go away.

Sad to say, it doesn't go away. We're all going to die, whether we plan properly for it or not. It's nobody's fault and it's certainly not the result of creating a will. Similarly, if we live long enough, we will reach retirement. If we don't plan properly, we won't have a very pleasant time of it in our later years. Those who fail to plan won't have many good choices and it won't be anyone's fault but their own.

Procrastination is the big pitfall. You must become informed and take action. If you don't, all you're going to do is make sure that there's plenty of additional work for people like me. I see people put off important decisions all the time because they don't want to deal with a sensitive topic or because of cultural beliefs. Either way, it's a serious mistake.

One reason why I respect Eric is that he genuinely cares about his clients and knows how to convince them to act. He has the knowledge and dedication to guide them past the many obstacles to successful planning, but he uses those talents in a way that helps ease his clients' concerns and realize their goals. Eric knows his clients well. He knows their dreams, their problems, and their families, not just their finances. He's constantly in touch with them, following up. That level of personal communication is something that has always amazed me. How he is able to keep so close to his clients and continuously monitor both the financial and the personal side of their lives is wonderful.

Virtually any financial advisor can tell you how your portfolio is performing or how this or that stock is doing. Eric sees the bigger picture. He understands that what is equally important is where you are in your life. What are your plans for the future? What are your needs right now? What's happening with your kids, your career?

I often tell financial planners that I'm envious of them. The planning business involves lawyers, accountants, bankers, insurance people and so forth. I view the whole thing as a big wheel. At the center of the wheel are the really good financial advisors like Eric. He gets it. The seminars we do together for his clients are a good example. He is constantly identifying potential issues for his clients so that they might benefit from bringing in an accountant or lawyer or insurance person. He's got the global view. He keeps his clients updated and monitors their progress. That's not easy to do. Not every financial advisor has that kind of dedication to stay close to their clients. It pays dividends and his clients love him.

People can sometimes be intimidated by the seeming complexity of the planning process as well as the perception of the Ivory Tower of the legal profession. Eric's very good at bridging the gap, getting people comfortable and teaming them up with lawyers and other financial professionals who will mesh with them.

He's also adept at helping clients see their own big picture. He helps them avoid tunnel vision or focusing too much on a single issue, such as avoiding probate. A lot of people are obsessed with the idea of having to avoid probate, but that's just one piece of the puzzle. I see people who latch onto the simplest solution to avoid probate, such as putting an asset into joint tenancy with their children. But if it's not done correctly it can open up a whole Pandora's Box of other issues. Sometimes action isn't the best course. Sometimes it's better to sit back and to think about it. Eric has the confidence and patience to advise clients to do that when he believes it's in their best interest. He's a great example of one of my mantras: "Act in haste, repent at leisure." Sometimes, you need to take some time and think soberly about these things before you move ahead. He's that voice of reason that helps you slow down and think things through properly.

Eric is really good at dealing with sensitive issues. At our seminars, we regularly hear people ask about passing assets on without getting into litigation. This can be a delicate issue, especially in families with more than one child. There seems to be a black sheep in every family. Here in B.C. we have legislation that allows people to challenge a will if they feel it doesn't provide for their proper maintenance and support. It's one of the broadest types of legislation across Canada. If parents decide to give a larger part of their estate to one child over another, the child who's been disadvantaged will often commence an action. It effectively freezes the estate until the matter is adjudicated. Eric is able to bring these delicate issues out in the open in discussions with his clients so they can find appropriate solutions. So often, planners and lawyers will simply ask people what they want to do with their assets and fill out basic documents. That may be fine in some isolated cases, but again, it can open up all kinds of problems after it's too late to do anything but go to court. Eric's close relationships with his clients allow him to explore these potential pitfalls and help find solutions to avoid them before it's too late.

When I meet with clients, I need all of their information about everything that has to do with their family dynamics — who's the black sheep, which kids have gotten loans, which kids don't get along with whom — before I discuss their assets. Even for a simple will it can be difficult to acquire all the necessary information. Some people are very private. I have to explain to them that I can't create the plan that is going to get them to where they want to get to unless I know all the details of their life. That's another reason why I appreciate Eric's attention to detail. When one of Eric's clients agrees to be referred to me, he makes sure I have all the necessary information, both in terms of assets and personal issues. He tells me about any potential red flags so I don't have to spend needless time trying to pull that information out of people. Obviously, they are comfortable sharing it with Eric so he can share it with me. It becomes a very efficient process that way.

There's no point going to a financial professional if you're not going to be forthcoming and candid. I think the people here in B.C. are well served by lawyers. It's difficult to become a lawyer here; we have a high standard of education. Most lawyers are very thorough but there remain some who have the "scribe" mentality. They simply ask for your name, the name of your beneficiaries, and create a will. It doesn't help people, but it's sure great for the litigators. It really sets the table for them later on.

It's so important for people to do their research and seek out advisors like Eric who are experienced and knowledgeable but retain the common touch. Many professionals don't understand that it's not about merely giving clients information. It's making sure to present it in such a way that they truly understand and can apply it to their circumstances. It's having open communication versus talking down to the client, which contributes to the procrastination and the Ivory Tower syndrome that keeps people from doing what needs to be done. Eric's very good at explaining things thoroughly and making sure people understand.

It's rewarding to hear people's comments at the seminars Eric and I conduct together. After twenty years, the reactions to our presentations are pretty much the same as they were when we first started.

People express their relief at finally being able to understand; the process is no longer a mystery. They are able to get their mind around it and see that they are not stuck, that there are solutions. They become excited to see that with some planning, they may actually be able to achieve what they want to achieve. For some, the breakthrough is sharing their experiences with others and learning that they're not alone. Many with problem children or other issues feel as though they have failed in some way and that they are different. They discover that the majority of families have similar issues.

The seminars help create a more positive attitude for these people. They feel empowered and come away with information they understand and can put to use. They feel they can now move forward. They are more comfortable talking with financial professionals and can more easily articulate what it is that they want. I very much enjoy doing these seminars with Eric. I find them personally rewarding because I deal with financial issues and terminology every day and it can get blasé. I know what a will and a power of attorney are. I know how trusts work. Clients will ask questions that come at issues from a totally different angle. I listen to their questions and realize I had never thought about it that way. Clients are always challenging us, forcing us to think in different ways and come up with different solutions. It's an exciting environment to be part of three or four times a year with Eric and I see the difference in people before and after the sessions. I think it's wonderful that Eric does this for his clients. I think he is an excellent financial advisor, as well as an excellent estate planner.

Eric's book explores the important issues surrounding retirement and estate planning and does it in a way that virtually anyone can relate to, understand and benefit from. It's time well spent and I recommend it highly.

Stephen M Miller
The Miller Law Group

Introduction

A 2013 survey revealed that 40 percent of retired Canadians had not prepared adequately for retirement; 54 percent said they've been unable to realize their retirement plans because they have less money to live on than they had expected.

Everyone hopes for an enjoyable retirement. But hope is a poor substitute for thoughtful planning and intelligent investment. I'm writing this book to help you gain a better understanding of the critical aspects of preparing for retirement. Just as important, I want to guide you past the many obstacles that can prevent you from reaching your goals.

I make the assumption that you are serious about planning for retirement. I also assume you are reading this book because you are not certain things are progressing as you would like them to regarding your retirement. Perhaps you have done some research on the Internet or engaged the services of a financial advisor. If you've spent time online, you may be confused by the vast amount of information available, much of which is contradictory. If you have an advisory relationship, you may be uneasy with the results or lack of communication. And if you rely on the media for financial expertise, you may be a victim of misinformation and hyperbole.

Obstacles to a successful retirement abound. In addition to circumventing information overload and distortion, you must manage your way through a minefield of Wall Street marketers, media talking heads, market analysts, prognosticators and a host of people within the industry whose livelihood depends on you repeatedly making emotionally driven financial decisions.

This is not to say everyone in the financial industry is out to get you but rather that by becoming more knowledgeable, you will be less likely to be distracted by misinformation and noise, and more apt to make intelligent planning and investment decisions. You will also be more confident that you are making the right choices to get you to where you want to be when you retire and beyond. I hope by reading this book you will become a smarter, calmer, more educated investor and ultimately achieve a truly rewarding retirement.

Experience is a Great Teacher

There isn't much I haven't experienced — good and bad — during my 28 years as an advisor. I clearly recall the market crash of 1987; the 1991-1993 recession when Canada was considered something of a banana republic due to its debt and deficit; the 1994 interest rate spike when bonds got crushed that spring; the 1998 Russian ruble and Southeast Asian currency crisis; the Mexican peso and Latin American debt fiasco; the Canadian real estate bust in the early 90s; the dot.com bubble and subsequent crash in 2000; the Enron and WorldCom debacles; Y2K; then 2007 and Bear Sterns going bankrupt; and the subsequent meltdown in 2008 when the markets froze, ultimately bottoming out in 2009. More recently came the European financial crisis of 2010-11. During all these events, I've continued to manage clients' investments and their financial futures. It has been a huge responsibility, something that cannot be learned by reading textbooks. It's knowledge acquired through persistence, working hard and smart through difficult times, ensuring clients won't panic and are kept informed.

Throughout the near unremitting turmoil of the past three decades, I've had the enormous satisfaction of helping investors calmly stay the course, avoid distractions and achieve a fulfilling retirement. Throughout the book, I'll share my experiences with you in the hope that you will learn from both the triumphs and disappointments.

Speaking of staying the course, do you remember how difficult it was to ignore the predictions of doom surrounding Y2K? There was worldwide panic over what might happen as a result of computers running amok. Would planes fall out of the sky? Would stock exchange computers suffer a meltdown and the markets crash? Would there be Depression-like runs on financial institutions? Would there be riots in the streets? Pat Boone built a bomb shelter in anticipation of the coming Armageddon.

A pre-2000 survey of 14,000 people conducted by the Gartner Group found that more than half planned to take two to six weeks' worth of cash out of their bank accounts and two-thirds planned to modify their stock investments.

The media did little to allay public fears. In fact, it took full advantage of the situation by dragging out pundits who predicted financial catastrophe...all in the interest of increased viewer ratings, of course.

Fifteen years later, the worldwide mania caused by Y2K seems almost surreal, but it was very real at the time and people who listened to all the noise made some ill-advised financial decisions as a result. Those who panicked and liquidated their stocks suffered a permanent loss when the markets rebounded once the computer glitches were fixed and it became apparent nothing horrible was going to happen.

A more recent example of perception overtaking sensibility involved financial "experts" repeatedly warning investors to sell their bonds because interest rates were about to spike. They've been spouting this for nearly three years now and guess which market sector outperformed last year? Yep: long-term government bonds!

You must be able to filter out the clamor. When misinformation abounds, when seemingly everyone around you is convinced that "this time it's different," you need someone who has been through it all before to remind you to keep your bearings and avoid overreaction to the noise. People who have reached their retirement goals by following this advice know this to be true. Once you finish reading this book, I believe you will too.

Chapter 1

Procrastination: Retirement Enemy Number One

"Only put off until tomorrow what you are willing to die having left undone."

$\approx$ *Pablo Picasso*

Many people defer planning for retirement, then one day wake up to find they are within a few years of retirement age and well short of the amount they will need to maintain their lifestyle. What to do? Is there some magical investment nostrum that can make up for their years of procrastination?

It saddens me to hear stories like this because there is no such investment, certainly nothing that can compensate for their inaction without taking unwarranted risks. Their misplaced focus on finding some exotic solution is a common response to the realization that delay has resulted in a looming retirement with few options.

Procrastination is, in my experience, the greatest threat to a satisfactory retirement. For those with limited means, it may be due to ineffective budgeting or the inability to defer gratification. Surprisingly, many with substantial wealth needlessly postpone retirement planning as well. Successful people sometimes believe their ability to earn money will take care of the problem and so pay little attention to the details in the years leading up to retirement. Whatever the motivation — or perhaps I should say lack of motivation — people on every rung of the economic ladder delay exploring a workable retirement strategy and taking action.

I know a couple — charming people with good intentions — who approach me from time to time with the intention of creating a plan for their retirement. Their annual earnings are in excess of $200,000 but now in their late forties, they have saved less than $100,000 for retirement. Each time we meet, they admit they have to save more and need a structured plan. When I remind them of our previous meetings where they committed to cutting back on expenses so they could begin saving more, they have an excuse as to why they couldn't follow through. They simply could not bring themselves to deal with the reality that time was growing shorter each year they delayed. I try not to give up on these people but fret that they will never get on with a plan until they are so close to retirement they can no longer ignore the issue. At that point, I fear they will be faced with the unpleasant option of delaying retirement or making some dramatic lifestyle changes.

People who procrastinate are susceptible to pitches for financial products promising unrealistic investment returns, not to mention all manner of financial schemes. Occasionally, we read about otherwise intelligent people who fall prey to some promotion and end up losing the money they do have. Too much of the financial industry emphasis is based on picking winners or timing the markets when for most people, the focus should be on planning and fundamentals.

The media and financial industry advertisers play a role in this. So much of what we see and hear from the media and financial industry revolves around <u>product</u>.

Financial news shows host investment managers who speculate on what the *hot stocks* will be for the coming year. Fund managers predict financial trends that invariably support their fund investment objectives. Hedge fund managers wax poetic about their enigmatic trading tactics. And all the while, the advertising campaigns of the companies employing these "experts" funnel huge sums into media coffers. It's an enormously lucrative, albeit incestuous, relationship: one that obviously pays off handsomely for both parties given its continuation.

People watch these messages and become convinced they can beat the market...make up for the years they failed to save for retirement. But the alluring investment products they hope will bring salvation are designed primarily to earn profits for the companies who create them, not to bail out those who have waited too long to start saving or who have been crippled by inappropriate investment choices.

A successful retirement strategy should <u>not</u> rely principally on investment performance. It should instead focus on creating a realistic retirement estimate, a commitment to follow the plan, and the confidence to ignore any distractions that may disrupt it. Ideally, all this should be attended to as early as possible. In others words, don't procrastinate!

> *"Procrastination is the art of keeping up with yesterday."*
> ≈ *Don Marquis*

In addition to delay, retirement planning can be devastated by the unforeseen. People tend to think of financial plans as roadmaps for how much money they will need to retire comfortably. Well, that's true, but a comprehensive plan will do more than merely tell you how much money you will need. It can also help plan for the variables — the unexpected little twists in life — that can inject unwanted stress into your retirement years.

Take the example of a man who joined a Canadian manufacturing company right out of college and through the years, worked his way up to senior vice president of marketing. He was loyal, competent and did everything right from a career perspective. One day the company was acquired by a conglomerate and shortly thereafter, he was let go. At age 57, he had never worked anywhere else. Despite his capabilities and experience, he was unable to find a comparable position anywhere else because of his age. Fortunately, we created a financial plan for him decades back and he followed it to the letter, so he had sufficient assets in his retirement account that he did not have to work any longer. While he was psychologically not ready for retirement and itched to get back into business, his situation could have been a financial disaster had we not planned for just such a contingency. He eventually adjusted to retirement; bought a motor home and he and his wife now travel around the country visiting their children and grandchildren at their leisure.

A change of company policy forced an executive at a large media company into retirement at age 65. Healthy, vibrant and loving his work, he planned to continue for many more years. He was financially secure and so didn't have to stress over finding another $250,000 position to support his and his wife's lifestyle, but being unexpectedly ousted is something no one can predict.

We can plan for the possibility, however.

In neither of these situations would the outcome have been as positive if we had not planned in advance and created options to address the unexpected. There's a big difference between unexpected and unprepared. Had these two executives delayed creating a comprehensive plan until later in life, there would not have been time to accumulate the funds necessary to safeguard them against unanticipated contingencies.

In the following chapters, I'll discuss other reasons to avoid procrastination, and examine how retirement plans are impacted by inflation, taxes, market risk and other factors.

Chapter 2

Taking Control

The trouble with retirement is that you never get a day off.

≈ *Abe Lemons*

Here's a startling fact from a 2012 McKinsey & Company study: "...over the past 30 years, life expectancy in Canada has increased by more than three years, while the average age of people entering the workforce increased by more than one year and the average retirement age decreased by more than two years. As a result, the ratio of years in retirement to working years grew from 36 percent in 1980 to 53 percent on average today."

Think of that. In Canada, the average life expectancy for a male born in 2012 is 80 and for females 84.[1] Assuming retirement at age 65, the average Canadian is expected to spend more than half as many years in retirement as he or she does working.

Here's another eye-opener from the same study. The demographic group least prepared to maintain their standard of living is not the young or middle aged; it's those within ten years of retirement. Equally surprising is the fact that those in the study's highest income bracket — earning an average of $140,000 annually — were the most vulnerable to outliving their money. The study suggests these people either failed to accumulate sufficient assets through workplace and individual savings or they accumulated too much debt to be properly prepared for retirement.

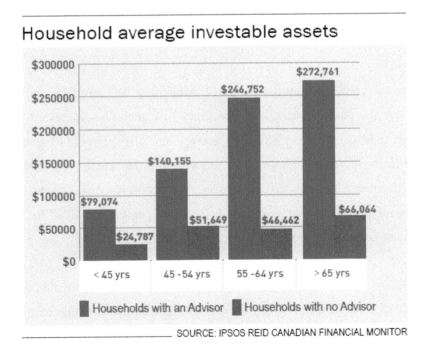

Household average investable assets

SOURCE: IPSOS REID CANADIAN FINANCIAL MONITOR

A 2013 Putnam Investment survey of 4,089 working people revealed that those working with a financial advisor were on track to replace 80 percent of their income in retirement. Those not working with an advisor were on track to replace just 56 percent.

The ability to replace income in retirement was not tied to income level but rather to savings level. Those who saved 10 percent or more of their income, no matter what the income level, were on track to replace *106 percent* of their income in retirement, which underscores the importance of consistent savings.

The difference in being able to replace 80 percent of your income versus 56 percent is significant. Using those numbers, a working couple earning $150,000 annually and working with an advisor could retire on $120,000 a year. The same couple without advisory help would retire on $84,000 a year. That would mean cutting back roughly $3,000 a month on expenses.

One of the obvious differences is that people with an advisor have someone other than themselves providing direction and fostering accountability. In short, a competent advisor will help you take the necessary steps that lead to a successful retirement.

The first step is commitment. You must assume a personal obligation to take control of your future. The best of intentions is meaningless without unwavering commitment.

You need a retirement roadmap, a path to get you from where you are to where you want to go. Not everyone needs an all-inclusive financial plan, however. For some, a financial estimate can suffice. I'll discuss this further in a later chapter.

Your retirement goals should be realistic and attainable. In my experience, people who set impractical goals tend to abandon their plan altogether once they realize they will fall short of their expectations. Better to plan conservatively and stick with it — or possibly overachieve.

Your goals should also be measurable so you will know if you are progressing as planned as you move closer to retirement. Having an experienced advisor monitor your progress and interpret whether you are on track can be helpful in this regard.

Take stock of your current situation. In meeting with prospective clients, I frequently discover they have only a vague idea of their net worth, not to mention what assets are held in their investment portfolio. Moreover, they often underestimate their debt and the cost of that debt. You have to know where you are before you can create a safe route to retirement.

Take responsibility for understanding financial fundamentals. Just as you can't ask your doctor intelligent questions unless you invest the time to learn about your body, you can't get the most out of working with an advisor if you don't know what to ask because you don't have a rudimentary understanding of how money works and other related financial matters. Make the investment to learn about investments, their risks and tax consequences.

If you want a glimpse of the importance of retirement planning, consider the impact of inflation. Let's assume you are presently 50 years old. Using a conservative estimate of 2% annual inflation, a pair of prescription eyeglasses that cost $250 day will cost roughly $340 when you retire. According to *Statistics Canada*, if you are age 65 and live where I do in British Columbia, you can expect to live another 20.7 years on average. Assuming also that your eyesight will continue to deteriorate as you age, when you go to buy eyeglasses in 30 years, at age 80, those specs will cost you $460.

If you extrapolate that amount to your total expenses, you can see that if you currently need $10,000 monthly to meet your obligations, in 30 years, you will need roughly $19,000 a month to maintain that lifestyle.

As an advisor, it's exciting to realize that creating a plan for someone exponentially increases their chances of being successful. I recall numerous instances where clients have achieved their retirement dreams by developing a plan and staying with it.

I met with one couple eighteen years ago: he a professor and she a university department fundraiser. They wanted to create a plan for a fulfilling retirement without financial worries. We discussed their circumstances and expectations and developed a course of action requiring they invest annually towards their retirement goal.

Eighteen years later, that couple is now happily retired. The professor is now a contented wood carver and bass guitar player (who would have thought?). His wife, the former fundraising lady, is now a marriage commissioner and loves the role. They don't have to fuss about money because it is being looked after, thanks to the plan we made eighteen years ago.

Chapter 3

Financial Obstacles

"Risk comes from not knowing what you're doing."
≈ *Warren Buffet*

A 2012 survey[2] indicated that 44% of Canadians ages 55 to 64 were not financially prepared for retirement. Only 53% had a long-term financial plan for retirement with three out of four feeling confident about their financial strategies. Among those without a plan, just 25% expressed confidence.

While most people understand the importance of developing a retirement plan, roughly half the population approaching retirement doesn't have one.

The road to a comfortable retirement is littered with potholes in form of economic, financial and personal obstacles. Each of us must travel this road and do our best to avoid the potholes that imperil our journey. Too many people choose to ignore them, relying on good fortune to guide them safely to their retirement destination. It makes no more sense than driving a car blindfolded, trusting providence to guide your travels.

The obstacles to retirement are numerous. The primary financial risks are inflation, taxes, market volatility, pension uncertainty, interest rates, sequence of returns and withdrawal rate. Lifestyle risks include but are not limited to health, longevity, employment or business continuity, bad advice and boredom.

Any of these can jeopardize your retirement, but the sheer number of obstacles and their unpredictability should have you questioning whether retirement is a journey you want to undertake without professional help.

Pension Risk

One of the least discussed but potentially most destructive obstacles is the reduction of employer pension plan benefits or worse, the loss of benefits altogether should the former employer go out of business. Many people have the mistaken notion that their employer pension plan benefits are guaranteed. In most cases, they are not. The neighbour of one of my clients was shocked recently when, seven years into retirement, his union pension plan benefits were slashed by approximately 35%. A relative of mine who spent his entire career working for a major warehousing company suffered a similar unanticipated reduction in pension benefits shortly after retiring. Those are just two of many such instances that have occurred.

According to an Aon Hewitt study of 449 Canadian defined-benefit pension plans from the public, semi-public and private sectors, plan solvency declined by nearly three percent in 2014, the first annual decrease since 2011. While no one can accurately predict plan solvency, the fact that it can suffer such a significant loss in just one year should give pause to currently employed workers who blithely rely on unwavering retirement income from their employer pension plans.

One glaring example of the unreliability of employer pension benefits is Canada Post, whose $6.5 billion pension shortfall represents a mere fraction of the more than $151 billion in unfunded government pension liabilities.[3]

Based on residency, Canadians qualify for Canada Pension Plan (CPP) and Old Age Security (OAS) benefits from the government. The amount of the CPP pension depends on the contributions made during a person's working years. For 2016, the maximum pension is approximately $1092 per month. CPP benefits are adjusted annually based on the Consumer Price Index and are included in total income for tax purposes. Benefits are designed to start at age 65 but a person can choose to begin receiving the pension earlier or later.

In recent years, the percentage of increase or decrease in the CPP retirement pension amount has changed. Prior to the change, those waiting to take CPP until age 70 prior received a pension amount 30% greater than those who took it at age 65. After 2013, the difference grew to 42% as a result of the change.

Other changes being implemented over a five-year period from 2011-2016 include:

> If you are under age 65 and work while receiving a CPP retirement pension, you and your employer will have to make CPP contributions. These contributions will increase your CPP retirement benefits.

> If you are age 65 to 70 and you work while receiving your CPP retirement pension, you can choose to make CPP contributions. These contributions will increase your CPP retirement benefits.

> The number of years of low or zero earnings that are automatically dropped from the calculation of your CPP pension will increase.

> You will be able to begin receiving your CPP retirement pension without any work interruption.

The maximum OAS pension benefit for 2016 is $570 per month and is taxable income. Retirees with sufficient income from other sources will see the government "clawback" some or all of their OAS benefits. For 2016, the minimum income recovery threshold is $73,756.

Currently, the OAS program appears to be reasonably solvent, but while the risks of reduced benefits may be lower than that with mandated CPP or optional employer funded pension plans, it still exists. And there is no guarantee that benefits or the income ceiling will not be lowered at some future time, possibly in response to the baby boomer infusion. The citizens of Mother Russia can attest to the unpredictability of government-funded benefit programs.

Inflation

Over the past one hundred years (1915-2014), the inflation rate in Canada averaged 3.2 percent.[4] Inflation has been modest in recent years, averaging about 2% annually, but occasionally it can rear its ugly head. When it does, the cost of even the most basic of life's necessities can dismantle retiree budgets. The ten years between 1973 and 1982 saw an average annual inflation rate of nearly 10%. While an obvious aberration, there's no assurance history won't repeat itself. Then too, the overall inflation rate may be modest, but selective goods or services may escalate at a much higher rate. For example, healthcare costs have risen much faster than the overall inflation rate in recent years. The seemingly incessant rise in healthcare costs is of particular concern to aging seniors.

Assuming average inflation of 3% per year, a retiree dollar at age 65 is only worth about 55 cents at age 85. Replacing a car purchased for $40,000 at age 50 will require over $72,000 at age 74.

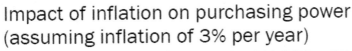

Impact of inflation on purchasing power (assuming inflation of 3% per year)

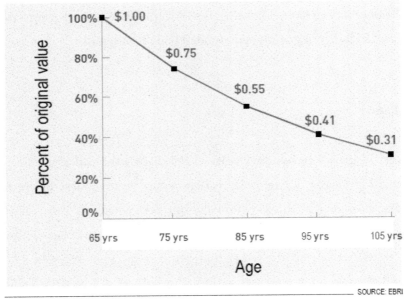

SOURCE: EBRI

Inflation is a retirement planning factor that most people seem to vaguely be aware of but not overly concerned about. Yet even at a modest rate of two or three percent a year, over time, it can have a dramatic impact on purchasing power. The table below shows the return necessary in order to net a 2 percent investment gain.

Combined income tax rate

Rate of inflation	Lowest bracket (27.37%)	Highest bracket (50.02%)
3%	6.88%	10.00%
4%	8.26%	12.00%
5%	9.64%	14.01%
6%	11.01%	16.01%
7%	12.39%	18.01%
8%	13.77%	20.01%
9%	15.15%	22.01%

SOURCE: THE MUIR INVESTMENT TEAM

Interest Rates

Many people overlook the fact that once they stop working, they will be dependent upon passive income to maintain their lifestyle. Typically, fixed income investments will represent a significant portion of their retirement portfolio's asset allocation. This is where interest rate risk lurks.

A low interest rate environment tends to reduce retirement income. More money must be accumulated during the working years leading up to retirement because retirees earn less income on fixed income investments such as bonds, GICs and term deposits. Low interest rates reduce bond payouts. Annuities purchased when interest rates are low yield less income at payout.

Conversely, when interest rates rise, the market value of existing bonds declines. Also, an adjustable-rate mortgage or credit card debt can accelerate rapidly.

Sequence of Returns

Retirement plan investment strategies typically utilize historical or average annual investment returns for their projections. For example, a plan might assume a 5 or 6% average annual rate of return, and indeed, that number might prove to be reasonably accurate over an extended period of time. As we all know, however, an average annual return is just that: an average. No intelligent person expects the market to deliver a nice, tidy 5% return every year. And given a healthy individual may logically expect to live 20 or 30 years after retiring, one may also logically expect there to be some significant variance in annual returns over that period.

The key is the timing of the returns. Poor investment returns early in retirement are much more damaging than poor returns later in retirement. This is referred to as the *sequence of returns* and it's important to understand its impact on the duration of a retirement portfolio. To illustrate this, consider the chart that follows. It's a hypothetical example of two portfolios entering retirement. Both begin with a balance of $500,000 and take $25,000 annual withdrawals, adjusted for 3% annually for inflation.

As you can see, after 30 years, the two portfolios have an identical average annual return of 6%, but Portfolio A suffered poor returns in the early years, whereas Portfolio B experienced most of its downside in later years. The difference is dramatic. Portfolio A exhausts its principle in year 13 — roughly age 78 for the retiree — whereas Portfolio B shows a balance of over one million dollars after year 13. Portfolio B not only continues to provide the needed annual withdrawals for the full 30 years, it also retains a principle balance of nearly one million dollars after generating some $58,000 in withdrawal income over the three decades.

Many retirees would be happy with a 3% annual withdrawal and an average annual return of 6% on their retirement portfolio. On paper, that sounds pretty good. But as the example illustrates, the timing of the returns can be more important than the overall average annual return.

ERIC MUIR

	DAVE AND JOAN				JEFF AND WENDY		

 DAVE AND JOAN Sequence of returns: Poor, then strong

 JEFF AND WENDY Sequence of returns: Strong, then poor

Hypothetical Net Return	Withdrawal	Balance	AGE	Hypothetical Net Return	Withdrawal	Balance
		$500,000	65			$500,000
-27.1%	$25,000	346,275	66	26.7%	$25,000	601,825
-16.5%	25,750	267,638	67	10.1%	25,750	634,259
-1.9%	26,523	236,535	68	4.3%	26,523	633,869
3.1%	27,318	215,702	69	8.9%	27,318	660,534
10.9%	28,138	208,009	70	17.6%	28,138	743,697
-9.4%	28,982	162,199	71	22.5%	28,982	875,527
7.4%	29,851	142,141	72	-3.7%	29,851	814,385
8.1%	30,747	120,417	73	18.1%	30,747	925,477
15.4%	31,669	102,415	74	-6.1%	31,669	839,286
9.4%	32,619	76,356	75	9.2%	32,619	880,880
6.2%	33,598	45,410	76	7.6%	33,598	911,675
12.4%	34,606	12,143	77	9.6%	34,606	961,268
2.8%	12,143	0	78	22.4%	35,644	1,132,964
11.4%	0	0	79	-11.0%	36,713	975,663
9.0%	0	0	80	24.3%	37,815	1,165,745
24.3%	0	0	81	9.0%	38,949	1,228,207
-11.0%	0	0	82	11.4%	40,118	1,323,532
22.4%	0	0	83	2.8%	41,321	1,318,113
9.6%	0	0	84	12.4%	42,561	1,433,720
7.6%	0	0	85	6.2%	43,838	1,476,055
9.2%	0	0	86	9.4%	45,153	1,565,407
-6.1%	0	0	87	15.4%	46,507	1,752,811
18.1%	0	0	88	8.1%	47,903	1,843,006
-3.7%	0	0	89	7.4%	49,340	1,926,397
22.5%	0	0	90	-9.4%	50,820	1,699,273
17.6%	0	0	91	10.9%	52,344	1,826,444
8.9%	0	0	92	3.1%	53,915	1,827,478
4.3%	0	0	93	-1.9%	55,532	1,738,278
10.1%	0	0	94	-16.5%	57,198	1,403,702
26.7%	0	0	95	-27.1%	58,914	980,350
Average Annual Net Return 6%				**Average Annual Net Return** 6%		

Public Policy

A frequently overlooked aspect of retirement planning is the potential for changes in government policies. Historically, tax increases have been an irresistible temptation for politicians seeking additional revenues to garner additional votes. Income, property and sales tax increases are almost a given. In addition, new types of taxes are likely, such as taxes on Internet purchases or consumption taxes. The precipitous drop in oil prices in the Fall of 2014 had some politicians mulling a hike in gas taxes.

It's virtually impossible to predict future changes in public policy. One thing we do know is taxes are almost never decreased or eliminated. Plan accordingly.

Chapter 4

Lifestyle Obstacles

"Take charge of your life! The tides do not command the ship. The sailor does."

$\approx$ *Ogwo David Emenike*

While the financial obstacles confronting a successful retirement may be more apparent, the personal or lifestyle obstacles, while often less obvious, are the factors over which we have greater control. It's important to recognize and address them because they have as great a potential to jeopardize your retirement as their financial counterparts.

You've no doubt heard the Serenity Prayer, *God grant me the serenity to accept the things I cannot change; courage to change the things I can; and wisdom to know the difference.*[5] That bit of insight certainly applies to lifestyle obstacles; they are the more controllable elements, assuming we have the foresight and courage to confront them.

Longevity

People are living longer than ever. Canadians have added 25 years to their lifespan in the last century. The average Canadian's life expectancy in 2014 is 81.7 years, up from 57 in 1921.[6]

Today, a 65 year-old male has a 50% chance of living to age 84 and a 25% chance of making it to age 90. Women age 65 have a 50% chance of living to age 87 and a 25% chance of making it to age 93. For married couples aged 65, there's a 50% chance at least one partner will live to age 90 and a 25% chance one partner will live to age 95.[7] As of this writing, there are over 6,000 Canadian centenarians. The financial implications of living a quarter century or more after retirement can be ominous.

The question virtually every person approaching retirement asks is, "Will I outlive my money?"

Clients often tell me they expect to live only until 80 or so, yet many find themselves approaching 90 and are surprised to be still among the living. Medical technology and an increased awareness of healthy habits has dramatically increased the percentage of people living well into their 90s and beyond. Just the other day I phoned a client to wish her a happy 90th birthday. My mom is a living testament to longevity. She's 89 and still running a bed and

breakfast in North Vancouver. She loves the guests and it keeps her
young.

Health

Retirement is ranked 10th on the list of life's 43 most stressful events.[8] A 2012 Harvard School of Public Health study of 5,422 seniors revealed that those who retired were 40% more likely to suffer a heart attack or stroke than those who kept working. The increase was especially pronounced during the first year of retirement.

The issue of deteriorating health in our later years is not so much a risk as it is a question of when, how swiftly and how seriously it declines. Many people I talk to about retirement assume their health will continue much as it is until the day they die. The various illnesses that afflict seniors may be an unpleasant topic but I sometimes have to remind clients that they are likely to be sick for some time before they die and they need to plan for that probability.

I hear people say they won't need as much income when they reach their 70s or 80s because they won't be as active or travel as much. But as a society, we are living longer and staying active longer. I enjoy riding my motorcycle and expect to continue doing so into my 80s. Why not?

As the huge baby boomer generation ages, it becomes increasingly dependent upon an already stretched healthcare system. Healthcare costs, currently a significant expenditure in provincial budgets, promises to become an incrementally more costly item in coming years. The effort to control costs has resulted in a shortage of physicians such that it commonly takes months to get a medical procedure scheduled. In addition, some preventative procedures previously recommended by the medical community — such as colonoscopies for men over age 50 — are now being discouraged, replaced by less expensive and potentially less effective tests.

Today's delays getting care at public facilities are well documented. Imagine the scenario ten or fifteen years from now as increased demand fueled by baby boomers further strains the healthcare system and its overworked professionals. I believe it is unavoidable that we will be paying considerably more for healthcare in the coming years, whether in the form of increased taxes to support public facilities or, for those who demand top quality healthcare without delay, the financial resources to pay for private facilities. The emergence of private clinics across Canada offering prompt, alternative healthcare is a harbinger of the future.

Changes in health can be sudden and unexpected. An accident, illness or even gradual deterioration linked to a chronic disease or cognitive impairment is not uncommon. Multiple problems tend to ensue when physical or mental capabilities decline. If family support is not nearby or available, a retiree lacking sufficient funding may well have to rely upon friends, neighbors or unreliable resources for assistance. It's an unpleasant alternative to family care.

The costs of long-term care are escalating rapidly. Just a few years ago, costs for long-term facilities typically ranged from $2,000 to $2,500 monthly. Today, that number is $4,000 to $5,000 monthly and rising.

A contributing factor, once again, is the lack of public facility construction. Sad to say, many of the existing government-sponsored facilities have long waiting lists. Quality facilities or caregivers are sometimes not available for acute or long-term care, even for private-paying individuals. When availability is low, families may select a facility or caregiver that turns out to be subpar. These facilities are not very nice places in which to spend one's final years, causing adverse consequences for both the family and the recipient.

Employment and Business Continuity

One of the risks every individual who works for someone else faces is the loss of employment. Companies downsize, merge or are acquired, with the result being a head count reduction. When unemployment strikes individuals in their fifties or sixties, it may be difficult to secure a comparable position or replicate income.

Those who plan to supplement their retirement income with part time work may find economic conditions preclude that option. They may not have the technical skills needed or discover available jobs are being filled by younger, lower cost workers.

Illness, disability or an accident can also occur forcing an early retirement with no possibility of replacing lost income.

A woman who worked in the veterinary field for her entire career was beset with health issues that made it impossible for her to fulfill her job responsibilities. She has since been looking for alternative employment for three years without success. She lives frugally and paid off her mortgage early, but without employment income, she relies on her dwindling savings and suffers the anxiety of an uncertain future.

The self-employed owner of a small retail shop became the victim of a discount chain that opened nearby. Forced to close his shop, he spent nearly a year looking for work before taking the only job available to him driving a school bus.

Business owners, professionals and other self-employed individuals ostensibly have greater control over their careers, but they are not immune to uncertainty when it comes to protecting their income.

Small businesses often lack succession plans. When the owner decides to retire, there's no assurance the intrinsic value of the business can be converted to hard assets through sale or continuity. Some small businesses and professions are entirely dependent on the talents of the owner or entrepreneur at the helm. Should that person become incapacitated or wish to retire, the viability of the business may be nonexistent.

Other, unforeseen elements may also come into play.

A client of mine, a 60 year-old woman with a thriving dental practice, decided to sell her practice and retire. She ran into a snag when the owners of the building where she leased space refused to give her a long-term lease because they planned to raze the building. Without a secure lease, her successful practice was worth substantially less. Luckily, the owners decided to sell the building instead of razing it and the new owners accommodated the dentist with an extended lease. She was able to sell her practice and retire as planned.

She was fortunate. Many others are not so lucky.

Withdrawal Rate

Poor performance in the early years of retirement can erode a portfolio's ability to generate income to last until death. Choosing an excessive rate of withdrawal is likely to have the same effect. Disproportionate withdrawals from a retirement portfolio run the risk of prematurely exhausting the principal, leaving nothing to generate income.

Several factors affect the selection of an appropriate withdrawal rate, including the portfolio's asset allocation (see graphic that follows), your capacity for risk, your discipline and willingness to adjust the rate if necessary, and your expected length of retirement, among others.

Percentage of simulations in which the portfolio was able to support all payouts and not run out of money prematurely.

	Annual Withdrawal Rate as (%) of Initial Portfolio Value						
	4%	5%	6%	7%	8%	9%	10%
Period	**100% U.S. Stocks**						
15 yrs	100	100	91	79	70	63	55
20 yrs	100	88	75	63	53	43	33
25 yrs	100	87	70	59	46	35	30
30 yrs	95	85	68	59	41	34	34
Period	**75% U.S. Stocks/ 25% Bonds**						
15 yrs	100	100	95	82	68	64	46
20 yrs	100	90	75	61	51	37	27
25 yrs	100	85	65	50	37	30	22
30 yrs	98	83	68	49	34	22	7
Period	**50% U.S. Stocks/ 50% Bonds**						
15 yrs	100	100	93	79	64	50	32
20 yrs	100	90	75	55	33	22	10
25 yrs	100	80	57	37	20	7	0
30 yrs	95	76	51	17	5	0	0
Period	**25% U.S. Stocks/ 75% Bonds**						
15 yrs	100	100	89	70	50	32	18
20 yrs	100	82	47	31	16	8	4
25 yrs	93	48	24	15	4	2	0
30 yrs	71	27	20	5	0	0	0
Period	**100% Bonds**						
15 yrs	100	100	71	39	21	18	16
20 yrs	90	47	20	14	12	10	2
25 yrs	46	17	15	11	2	0	0
30 yrs	20	17	12	0	0	0	0

SOURCE: THE MUIR INVESTMENT TEAM

Occasionally, retirees will express the desire to withdraw more than I recommend based on their individual circumstances. For clients age 65 and older, I typically suggest not exceeding a 6% annual withdrawal rate as it tends to deplete principal too quickly. But when markets perform well over an extended period, retirees can forget that markets move down as well as up. When the stock market plunges, retirees without professional guidance may panic and move their investments out of the market and into the perceived safety of GICs or similar fixed income investments. The trouble with that type of kneejerk reaction is that you can't withdraw even 6% a year for long if your portfolio consists of GICs yielding just 2-3%.

External Influences

All investors are subjected to the unrelenting assault of external influences: financial product marketers, commissioned salespeople, brokers, 24/7 financial and news media, family members, friends, business associates, con artists and other predators. Collectively, they create a lot of noise that can be hard to ignore.

Retirees can be especially vulnerable to the noise because most seniors have stopped working and now rely on passive income to support their lifestyle throughout retirement. As they advance in years, they may suffer a decline in judgment, making them even more susceptible to outside influences. Advice from family members may be well intentioned, but often those offering counsel are no more financially astute than the elders they seek to help. Caregivers with poor intentions may take advantage of a trusting elder. Financial salespeople and brokers may encourage retirees to purchase inappropriate investment products. A retiree's combination of accumulated wealth and declining cognitive abilities can be an irresistible temptation for dishonest practitioners, as some of the victims of Bernie Madoff learned.

In 2011, 90 year-old actor Mickey Rooney was granted court protection from two stepchildren who were accused of taking control of his finances, blocking access to email and even denying him basic necessities such as food and medicine.

"All I want to do is live a peaceful life, to regain my life and be happy," Rooney wrote. "I pray to God each day to protect us, help us endure and guide those other senior citizens who are also suffering."

I have had a few senior clients experience pressure from family members to give them money because they couldn't manage their own money prudently. One of the advantages of having a trusted financial advisor is that we can be of tremendous support when undue pressure is exerted on a client by wayward children or others.

It's easy to see how any of these external influences can throw a retirement plan off course by distorting reality or causing retirees to question their financial strategy.

Chapter 5

Behavioural Obstacles

"It's not what happens to us, but our response to what happens to us that hurts us."

≈ *Stephen R. Covey*

As previously mentioned, we have greater control over personal obstacles than economic obstacles when it comes to planning for retirement. There is, however, another obstacle to successful retirement that virtually everyone shares to a greater or lesser degree: our behavior. Each of us has ongoing difficulties with behavioral issues in one form or another. Our behavioral instincts dictate *how we react* as investors to personal, financial and external influences, which has a profound impact on whether we achieve our retirement goals.

A great deal of research has been done in the area of investor behavior and much of it illustrates why individual investors tend to underperform market averages by a significant margin. In this chapter, I cite a number of studies on investor behavior. The findings reinforce my own three-decade empirical experience relating to investor behavior.

As an example, a study by Brad Barber and Terrance Odean[9] provides some fascinating insights into individual investor behavior, among them:

> ➢ Many individual investors hold under-diversified portfolios, and trade actively, speculatively, and to their detriment.

> ➢ Investors tend to sell winning investments while holding on to their losing investments — a widely observed behavior dubbed the "disposition effect." It's a reluctance to sell a stock that has lost money. By not taking a loss, investors can avoid responsibility for their mistakes. The disposition effect also tends to maximize taxes because selling winners generates a tax liability that might be deferred simply by selling a losing, rather than winning, investment. *How many investors refused to sell Nortel, Ballard Power or Blackberry stocks as they continued to plunge downward?*

> ➢ Where people live contributes to their behavior. Investors tend to hold stocks of companies close to where they live and invest heavily in the stock of their employer. These behaviors

lead to an investment portfolio containing unnecessarily high levels of risk. *This is often referred to as "familiarity bias."*

> The media influences investors. The attention-based buying of stocks can lead investors to trade too speculatively and has the potential to influence the pricing of stocks. *By the time individual investors hear about a stock in the news, it's already old news.*

The study concludes that investors who inhabit the real world and those who populate academic models are distant cousins. In theory, investors hold well-diversified portfolios and trade infrequently so as to minimize taxes and other investment costs. In practice, investors behave differently. They trade frequently and have perverse stock selection ability, incurring unnecessary investment costs and return losses. They tend to sell their winners and hold their losers, generating unnecessary tax liabilities. Many hold poorly diversified portfolios, resulting in unnecessarily high levels of diversifiable risk, and many are unduly influenced by media and past experience. Individual investors that ignore the prescriptive advice to buy and hold lower-fee, well-diversified portfolios generally do so to their detriment.

According to *Psychonomics,* an organizational development and investment behavior consultant, "Behavioral finance researchers show, scientifically, that investors do not always act rationally or consider all of the available information in their decision-making process. As a result, they regularly make errors. It turns out too that the errors they make are repeated in the same way, and are, therefore, termed *systematic errors*. Luckily, because of this systematic character, these errors are often predictable and avoidable. Nevertheless, psychologically determined, they continue to occur frequently in stock markets and are made by both novice and professional investors alike."

This supports the argument for employing an experienced financial advisor.

Extrapolation Bias

The markets are rarely as good or as bad as investors perceive. But *extrapolation* can cause investors to conclude otherwise. It can be defined as the tendency of investors to project recent events or conditions into the future. It's the basis for investors convincing themselves that a short-term trend will continue indefinitely. The misperception can lead to inaccurate or poorly timed investment decisions. In some cases, it leads to a debilitating loss of investment principle.

A convincing example of this is the month of December 2014. Oil was trading at over $100 a barrel and most investors here in Canada extrapolated that it was destined to remain at that level or go higher. When oil prices suddenly nosedived, sending oil industry stocks plummeting, the many investors who regarded oil industry issues as a continuing sure bet were caught overexposed to the sector and saw their holdings drop by 40-50% or more virtually overnight.

A record profit earnings report by Apple in January 2015 sent the stock price soaring roughly 8% in a matter of hours. I was immediately reminded of the many times in the past that investors regarded a stock or market sector as an unsinkable ship, only to later see it submerge beneath the waves.

People with knowledge or skills in other areas, such as sports, medicine, entertainment or business sometimes extend their confidence into believing they are equally competent investors. It's one reason why we frequently read about celebrities or professional athletes being duped by investment hucksters. That publicity does not dissuade financial product advertisers from utilizing these luminaries to tout their products.

According to Peter Andresen, "If an active trader sits down and reflects, he or she is likely to choose a less turbulent form of investing. To avoid such an onset of rationality, brokerage advertisements feature actors who appear to be competent, successful, beautiful people and imply that such accomplished professionals are also competent at investment management. They are aiming straight at your vulnerability for ego extrapolation."[10]

Anchoring Bias

Another major bias is anchoring, the overreaction to or fixation on past information and using that to make inappropriate investment decisions.

The CFA Institute's Robert Stammers notes, "When investors are influenced by this bias, they may not be able to get their mind off a particular sell-price target, even if new information is available or the investing landscape has shifted significantly. They become stuck and may even ride markets to the bottom if they cannot let go of what they think the price 'should' be."[11]

How often do we hear investors say they will sell a loser once the stock bounces back to what they paid for it? How many investors — even supposedly knowledgeable institutional investors — hung on to their Polaroid, Xerox or Kodak stocks, waiting for them to rebound as they slid inexorably into a black hole? I must sometimes remind investors they don't know the price they paid for the sinking stock they refuse to sell.

Anchoring can distort clear thinking because it creates a point of reference — or anchor — for the investor's emotions.

Home Bias

The term home bias refers to the tendency of investors to hold financial investments in their home country versus foreign markets. A 2012 Vanguard study highlights the propensity for investors to overweight their portfolios in domestic securities. Canadians are especially susceptible to home bias. The graphic that follows approximates a country's home bias by comparing investment by domestic investors in domestic securities to the percentage weighting of each domestic market in the global market. The size of each bubble indicates domestic security overweighting. So while U.S. investors held 29 percentage points more U.S. equities than the U.S. market capitalization, Canadians held a whopping 60% more Canadian stocks that the Canadian market capitalization. The domestic overweighting for fixed income investments was even higher.[12]

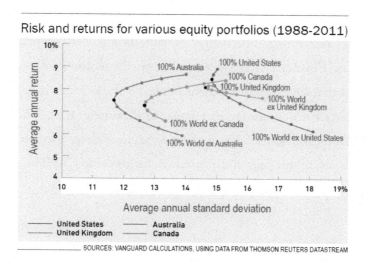

Risk and returns for various equity portfolios (1988-2011)

SOURCES: VANGUARD CALCULATIONS, USING DATA FROM THOMSON REUTERS DATASTREAM

Among the key drivers of home bias, the Vanguard research paper identifies:

> ➢ Expectations about future returns in their home markets;
> ➢ Preference for the familiar, even if it results in poorer risk-return trade offs;
> ➢ Higher costs to access foreign securities, and;
> ➢ Perception that foreign investments are inherently more risky.

One explanation among the many explored by a host of research papers over the decades is that investors tend to feel more confident about their own country's prospects. Another possible reason for home bias is that people are more familiar with and cognizant of financial, economic and political conditions in their own country. A study published in the *Journal of Psychology and Financial Markets* reinforces the strong bias for domestic stocks[13] as test groups of investors expressed greater confidence in domestic stocks.

Another interesting observation about home bias appeared in European Financial Management, where the authors of a study[14] observed that investors overweight domestic stocks in their portfolios in proportion to consumption relative to their neighbors. They note that, "Domestic stocks are preferred because they also serve the objective of mimicking the economic fortunes and welfare of the investor's neighbors, countrymen and social reference group."

As a personal observation, perhaps investors' preference for domestic stocks is not unlike a similar penchant among investors with employer-sponsored pensions to overweight their portfolios with stocks of the companies they work for. Confidence tends to run higher in things with which they are familiar. Telus employees are a good example of that.

Investors Do Worse than Market Averages

Over the 20 years ending 12/31/2009, the average investor experienced investment returns significantly lower than those generated by a passive, non-managed portfolio of S&P 500 stocks, according to the investment research firm Dalbar. The annualized return of an average equity investor during the two decades was 3.17% compared to an annualized return of 8.20% for the S&P 500 index. A subsequent Dalbar study of the 20 years ending 12/21/2011 revealed similar findings:

A report by the investment research company, Morningstar®, found that investors also experienced significantly lower returns than were earned by the very funds they were invested in. Morningstar® found that because of the timing of investors' purchases and sales of fund shares, investors performed worse than if they had simply held the fund through good and bad times.[15]

20-year annualized returns by asset class (1995 – 2014)

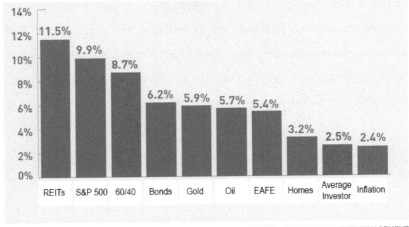

SOURCE: MORNINGSTAR DIRECT, DALBAR INC., J.P. MORGAN ASSET MANAGEMENT

Herd mentality helps explain why investors do worse than the investments they hold. Paul Kofman, Professor of Finance at Melbourne University, adds that the phenomenon of cognitive bias[16] contributes to the herd mentality: "When the market is surging investors will flock to it, expecting ever more unrealistic gains and allocating their portfolios accordingly. When the inevitable downturn follows, investors will turn increasingly pessimistic yet surprisingly hold on to their risky portfolios to avoid capitalizing losses. When they finally reallocate their portfolios to low-risk cash investments, they subsequently refuse to respond to a market turnaround."

> *"What we believe is heavily influenced by what we think others believe."*
>
> ≈ *Thomas Gilovich*

History shows that mutual fund investors generally increase inflows after observing periods of strong performance. They buy at high prices when future expected returns are lower, and they sell after observing periods of poor performance when future expected returns are now higher. This results in what author Carl Richards called the "behavior gap," in which investor returns are well below the returns of the funds in which they invest. Perhaps with this observation in mind, Warren Buffett once said, "The most important quality for an investor is temperament, not intellect."[17]

I recall February 2000, a classic month for stock market inflows. It was the height of the technology bubble and the majority of investors believed the bull market would continue indefinitely. But that ended up being the peak of the market. The tens of thousands who thought technology stocks, many with 50 or higher P/E ratios, would continue climbing to never-ending heights had their overweighted portfolios clobbered when the tech bubble burst.

So many investors struggled with their behavior during the dot.com era. I remember the challenge of trying to respond rationally to the many clients who questioned why we were not buying more technology and telecom company stocks for their portfolio prior to the bubble bursting. I kept trying to reassure our investors that the tech stocks they were imploring me to buy were overpriced and didn't have the intrinsic value to justify their inflated prices. The majority of our clients listened, took my advice and it paid off handsomely for them when the inevitable downturn occurred. The few that didn't lost a sizable amount of money.

As they are during most market runups and downturns, the news media was one of investor's worst enemies, feeding the buying frenzy well past the point when values made any sense, and warning investors of impending doom after the market had already begun to rebound.

Periodically, someone will send me a report some analyst or TV journalist has created that solemnly predicts doom and gloom or overhypes a risky or unsustainable investment idea. It's my role to be the voice of reason and help clients stay on the straight and narrow when they become enamored with these inappropriate investment fantasies. Sometimes, my greatest value to my clients is to prevent them from making mistakes.

Chapter 6

Widow and Divorcee Issues

The issues facing widows and divorcees are among the most overlooked financial topics. Everyone who marries hopes for a lifelong relationship but as we know, that isn't always the case. In 2008, the last year for which *Statistics Canada* provided divorce information, the percentage of marriages projected to end in divorce was an astounding 40.7%! The average age at divorce was 44.5 years for men and 41.9 years for women. The ratio of female lone-parent families to male lone-parent families is four to one.[18]

For female seniors, the likelihood of being single at some point during retirement is higher because women tend to marry older men and live an average of five years longer than men. The average age of widowhood for women in Canada is just 56. *Census Canada* data shows that 43% of Canadian seniors are single.

According to a study by the *UN Platform for Action Committee Manitoba*, after a divorce, a woman's income drops an average of 45%. The study's statistics show half of single women over the age of 65 live in poverty and half of married women would live in poverty without their husband's income. The study also reports that widows accounted for 45 percent of all women aged 65 and over.

After five years of widowhood, median income among senior women typically declines 9.8 percent, more than six times greater than the 1.5% decline among senior women who do not become widows.[19]

In general, women tend to live longer than men, spend fewer years working and earn less income. According to a Status of Women Canada study of real average earnings of full-time workers age 15 and older, men earned an average of $62,690 annually as compared to women who earned an average of just $44,700.

Even when divorce or widowhood is not a factor, married women are too frequently omitted from serious financial discussions or advisory meetings. Happily, that trend appears to be changing. One reason is that increasingly, women are taking a greater interest in their family's financial futures and are more knowledgeable about money-related topics. Also, more women than ever hold management and executive positions. These women tend to have more financial acumen but may be so busy with their careers or with running a business that they neglect to take precautions to safeguard their assets and estates. If the woman is the family's breadwinner, she must take into account what would happen if she became incapacitated and was unable to generate income.

I do my best to include both spouses in any financial planning or investment review sessions I conduct with my married clients. I believe it's important for both spouses to be involved, not only so they become more familiar with planning and investment matters, but also that should one of them die unexpectedly, they have a foundation of knowledge upon which to make sound financial decisions.

Too often in the past, even when wives participated in financial meetings, many had little more than perfunctory input. Being left out in the cold, so to speak, can have tragic consequences when a marriage ends, particularly if the husband was the exclusive or primary source of family income. Suddenly without their financial bedrock, women can face frightening monetary uncertainty, not to mention debilitating emotional stress.

A few weeks ago, the wife of one of my long-time clients called to tell me he had died suddenly of a massive heart attack. It was a horrible shock. He was 57 years old, a happily married dentist, seemingly in good health, not overweight nor stressed. One of those deaths that make you scratch your head, not to mention frightening on a personal level.

His wife, a homemaker, is a lovely, gentle person. She is suddenly facing the prospect of a life without her loving husband, who made virtually all the couple's financial decisions. I always try to get clients to include their spouses in our financial meetings but, of course, as the advisor, I can't insist on it if a client chooses not to do so for whatever reason. This was one of those instances where the wife, who is originally from Japan, felt more comfortable leaving all the financial, investment and business practice decisions up to her husband. She must now contend with the unexpected and unfamiliar task of selling her husband's dental practice. She must also contend with locating and organizing all the couple's financial documents and paperwork.

Can you imagine having to deal with the emotional distress of losing one's spouse at such a young age without any warning and simultaneously trying to quickly recuperate something from his lifetime of work before his patients find another dentist and the practice no longer has value?

At his funeral, I heard many people comment on how shocked they were that someone who took such good care of himself could die so suddenly. It brought home the reality of what I tell my clients regarding planning for the unexpected, having one's will, power of attorney, health directives and other important estate paperwork updated and organized. I also emphasize the importance of including one's spouse in the financial and estate planning process so that should the unforeseen occur, the spouse is not left scrambling for documents and forced to make financial decisions in a traumatized environment. This is not hypothetical rhetoric; death and disability happen. Sadly, they happen all too frequently to those unprepared.

After numerous instances of seeing clients pass away without having all their important documents organized, our firm embarked on the task of creating a bound booklet for each client that can be filled out with all of his or her financial particulars. This way, if something happens, there is an organizational document that provides the spouse, executor or trustee with all the information relating to advisors, investment accounts, properties, insurance coverage, wills, legal documents and contacts for each. It will save time and make getting through the process so much easier for those left behind.

Making sound decisions under such trying circumstances can be almost impossible, especially if the woman was not privy to the overall financial condition of the family. What if the available assets won't safely generate sufficient income to support her lifestyle? What options does she have? If she had a professional career but has been retired for any length of time, getting back into active practice can be difficult. If she is a senior without a career, finding anything but menial or tedious work can be problematic. The alternatives to returning to the workforce include lowering her standard of living or investing more aggressively. Neither may be an attractive option.

The logical solution for women is to begin taking a more inclusive approach to the family's financial affairs. Taking the first step can be intimidating for women who have not previously been part of financial decisions. A variety of reasons may cause a partner to not be involved. Husbands may sense their financial acumen is being challenged. If a husband was previously married, there may be an ex or children from the marriage with a financial interest and the second wife may be perceived as trying to gain financial control for personal reasons. It can become a knotty issue. But these obstacles should never prevent a woman from becoming more involved in family finances and investment decisions.

What are the first steps a couple should take to make sure the wife is protected in case her husband dies or becomes disabled? Certainly there should be adequate life and disability insurance, a comprehensive estate plan, power of attorney, appropriate healthcare paperwork, the existence of any pension, deferred profit sharing plan (DPSP), employer benefits or stock options, and knowledge of where all the related papers are located. She should also know if there are any arrangements or obligations from a previous marriage that would impact the estate or trigger probate.

While things have changed for the better and in general, women are more cognizant of financial issues, it distresses me that so many women still remain on the sidelines when it comes to being prepared for the unexpected, whether it be a divorce or the death of their spouse.

Married women would be wise to confront the "what if" factor before faced with the reality of divorce or the death of their husband. They should have a realistic plan for how to make up for lost income and pay for ongoing expenses. They should know where to find all financial information, including bank, credit card, retirement and investment accounts. It's also critical to have easy access to wills, insurance policies and tax records. Power of attorney, representation agreements and healthcare directive forms should be signed so a woman has the ability to make necessary decisions about assets held in joint tenancy with her deceased or incapacitated spouse.

I believe creating these documents and having access to them is so important, our firm conducts a semi-annual estate planning course for our clients and other interested parties.

Compiling a checklist of documents is a good idea. Also, the names of all the family's professional advisors should be readily available. In addition to any necessary paperwork and documentation, contact information for each account, advisor and organization should be maintained and regularly updated.

In the case of a death, particularly a sudden unexpected death, surviving spouses may suffer debilitating stress. In such circumstances, it might be wise for the widow to defer as many significant decisions as possible. While some matters must, by necessity, be dealt with promptly, others can be postponed until a less stressful time.

Pressure may exist to make quick decisions but the repercussions can be costly. Having a trusted advisory relationship can help a widow determine what needs to be done immediately and what can be postponed for a while. The advisor can also be a source of comfort for a distressed widow and help alleviate anxiety over financial decisions.

Chapter 7

Media Madness

"If you don't read the newspaper, you're uninformed. If you read the newspaper, you're misinformed."

≈ *Mark Twain*

A study published in the *Journal of Financial Economics*[20] determined that media coverage not only influences investor behaviour, it intensifies behavioural biases like extrapolation and anchoring (see previous chapter).

Writing in *Fiduciary News* about media coverage of retirement issues, Christopher Carosa notes mass media reporters, while perhaps well-trained journalists, often lack the relevant experience to do justice to retirement topics. He believes the over-simplification can lead to potentially hazardous generalizations about investing.[21]

There's little argument that the mass media has a huge impact on the investment decisions made by individuals. The tone of the media's reporting also plays a key role in determining investor sentiment. In a research paper on the subject, Paul Tetlock[22] measures media interactions with the stock market. He finds that when the media is highly pessimistic, market prices trend downward. He also finds that unusually high or low pessimism in the media precedes elevated market trading volume.

Tetlock's research included a 15-year, word-content analysis of the *Wall Street Journal's* "Abreast of the Market" column. He found a direct correlation between a rise in the number of pessimistic words in the column and a market downturn the next day. *Canadian Business* writer Larry MacDonald interprets Tetlock's view thusly: "...professional investors have their own sources of information such that they usually know about the information before it gets published in the media. Readers of the media are thus reacting to *stale data*, causing an overshoot in prices. After they drive the prices of mentioned stocks up or down, sophisticated investors will return prices to their fundamentals by buying the stocks experiencing media-induced dips and/or shorting the stocks with media-induced spikes."

None of that bodes well for average investors who are unaware they are on the outside looking in when they respond to positive or negative hype from the mass media. What they hear from the media is typically either old or hyped information, neither of which is conducive to making informed investment choices.

Investors who act on information they glean from the media believe they are getting accurate, timely information. If they didn't, they wouldn't pay any attention. The media knows they must purport to be delivering credible information and so they parade an endless procession of analysts, economists, fund managers and other "experts" who are given name recognition and exposure in exchange for providing "inside" information. The real dope is the investor who listens and acts on the speculation without questioning the motives of the person offering the advice.

Consider why an analyst or manager at a Wall Street investment firm would appear on a financial news show and offer to share their knowledge about specific issues for free. What is their motivation? Perhaps they believe that viewers who act on their advice and make money will become clients of their firm. That's not an unreasonable assumption. If enough viewers buy the stock, the price is likely to rise.

A study published in the *Journal of Finance* reveals that a portfolio of stocks without media coverage outperforms a portfolio of stocks with significant media coverage by 3% annually, after adjusting for market size, book-to-market, momentum and liquidity.[23] The study found that mass media could affect security pricing even if it does not supply genuine news."[24]

Another aspect of financial news — or any news reported by the media for that matter — is the need to keep viewers glued to their televisions. That can't be accomplished by advising investors to formulate a plan and stick to it, to buy quality stocks and hold them for the long term, to ignore the noise and distractions fomented by those with motives not necessarily in the best interests of viewers. Heck, that would be a self-indictment of the very strategies the media uses to keep viewers and listeners tuning in. People want excitement and stimulation. They want to believe they are privy to expert knowledge that will help them beat the market. They should know better but they don't act that way. The media knows viewers will be bored to death with substantive, tried-and-true investment knowledge. So while the media may occasionally pay lip service to investing for the long term and having a good plan, they know people respond to appeals to their primitive investment emotions: fear and greed. That's what the media provides and sad to say, it is highly successful...for the media, the talking heads and the financial product producers and marketers whose advertising dollars keep the media alive.

The effect of 24/7 financial news reporting is to keep viewers on edge about their investments. "Am I missing an opportunity to get in on the next dot.com? Should I put some money into emerging markets? Is international investing too risky; should I get out? Is that analyst right when he says my bonds are going to be worth nothing when interest rates rise? That fund returned 15% last year; should I jump on the wagon? Oil prices have plummeted but people will always need oil, won't they? Is now the time to buy oil stocks? That actor who talks about inflation and the safety of precious metals? Should I be buying gold?"

Again, the media loses its audience (and its advertisers) if people adhere to a passive strategy and simply hold onto their good investments for the long term. When media hype or doom and gloom carries the day, investors become rattled and uncertain about their strategy. All the calm, reasoned thinking that went into their plan for retirement investing goes out the window in a flash. They lose confidence that they are doing the right thing. They ask friends for advice, people who know nothing more than they do. They become even more confused. They are whipsawed by conflicting reports from talking heads with their own agendas. The media has become one of the least reliable sources of financial information. The media is all about the hype, the noise. They have to keep your attention and so they play on your basic emotions: fear and greed. And they know bad news is more likely to motivate you to act than good news. It's no place to go for serenity or encouragement.

> *The newspaper journalists like to believe the worst; they can sell more papers that way, as one of them told me himself; for even upstanding and respectable people dearly love to read ill of others."*
>
> ≈ *Margaret Atwood*

An experienced advisor who has been through one or more full economic cycles can provide the calm voice of reason needed to keep investors on track. Most people don't think about that when they engage an advisor but it is precisely when market turbulence is at its worst that jittery investors need the reassurance and savvy of a seasoned financial professional, not the blather of the mass media.

> *"The smallest bookstore still contains more ideas of worth than have been presented in the entire history of television."*
>
> ≈ *Andrew Ross*

I recall reading about a study of the murder rates in Florida a few years ago. People were asked if they thought the murder rate had gone up or down during the previous 20 years. Respondents overwhelmingly said it had gone up. But in fact, the murder rate had declined by nearly 50%. The reporting of murder had quadrupled, however, creating the perception that murders were on the rise. Increased reporting was the only discernable difference.

Similarly, the emergence of the 24/7 news cycle, internet access and social media have combined to elevate the level of "news noise" that creates the impression that more is happening than actually is. The impressionable investing public becomes convinced that "this time is different" when it isn't. The impact of media noise is yet another reason why investors typically do worse than the fund they invest in. Perception is a powerful thing. Listening to the wrong information creates the wrong perception, which in turn can eviscerate an otherwise healthy investment portfolio.

The mass media exists to sell advertising and make money for its investors. It does not exist to educate the public about sound investment principles. Be wary of any financial advice you get from the media. The media is not your friend.

Chapter 8

Advisor Intangibles

"Every treasure is guarded by dragons. That's how you can tell it's valuable."

≈ *Saul Bellow*

There is no foolproof way to totally circumvent the financial, lifestyle and behavioral obstacles that stand between you and your financial goals. There are, however, preemptive strategies available that can mitigate their impact and increase the odds of fulfilling your aspirations.

Some of these strategies are fundamental in nature and require little more than a commitment to change attitude or behavior. Some are more sophisticated and require the financial savvy of an experienced financial professional.

Let's consider some of the more important tactics as they relate to overcoming the obstacles that stand in the way of achieving your goals.

Longevity

Obviously, we don't know the date when our time on the planet will come to a halt. What we do know is that as a society, we are staying healthier and living longer than our ancestors. And the longer we live, the more we need to plan for an extended period beyond our working years. The challenge is to provide an adequate income stream for an unpredictable period of time.

The uncertainty of the markets complicates the investment component of planning for our future. Uncertainty can't be eliminated but a well thought out plan, appropriate asset allocation and timely rebalancing can go a long way towards securing a satisfying retirement and late life.

A trusted advisory relationship can help mitigate the mental anguish that often accompanies a severe market downturn. Nothing can completely eradicate the psychological uneasiness of seeing the value of your portfolio decline, but an advisor whose clients have weathered previous bear markets can help you manage your emotions and avoid making rash financial decisions.

The challenge is managing the market's inherent volatility, both financially and psychologically. Your advisor should communicate with regularity, keeping you informed of what is happening, especially during difficult times. That may sound like a given, but some advisors avoid communication when times are bad, hoping client silence means acquiescence. Assuming your portfolio contains quality investments, your advisor should be the voice of reason, offering reassurance to stay the course, that "this time is not different," that ultimately, your investments will recover and resume their growth. You really don't realize how important having a calm voice of reason to rely on is until the markets swoon and panic sets in.

That's when the intangible value of a competent advisor becomes more evident. It's also a reason why studies indicate investors who have an advisory relationship fare better than those who do not, according to Dalbar. In the research firm's 2014 *Quantitative Analysis of Investor Behavior*, it observes,

"Investors may only have themselves to blame...(they) make poor investment choices that hurt their investment returns. These decisions, including when to buy and sell, are often driven by emotion."

"Price is what you pay. Value is what you get."
≈ *Warren Buffett*

Health

We are all more aware of healthy habits and their effect on our longevity nowadays. I doubt you need or want your advisor to counsel you on diet, exercise or other health factors. But I believe as an advisor, I can add value to my services by providing my clients with access to information about lifestyle, financial and other related topics. I do this by sponsoring monthly seminars and workshops where experts from various disciplines speak and interact with my clients.

A recent seminar on aging was attended by some 200 clients and guests. The speaker was a noted physician who provided tips on aging well. Other seminars included an economist who assessed the previous year's markets; a tax season session with the head of tax planning for Raymond James; another session with a tax attorney examining the issues surrounding cross-border tax planning; a workshop featuring a local estate planning attorney; another exclusively for women on financial planning; and presentations by a variety of portfolio managers.

The topic of aging well has no direct connection with my business of planning and investment management, but it does relate to the overall well-being of my clients, as do many of the other subjects covered at our events. By providing expert information and an inviting atmosphere, I feel I am making it more likely my clients will receive the kind of practical knowledge that helps them be better educated and consequently, enjoy a better lifestyle.

When interviewing a potential advisor, you probably never thought about asking whether he conducts workshops on financial and lifestyle topics, but added services like this indicate a professional commitment to provide a holistic advisory experience.

Business Continuity and Employment

The financial advantages and personal fulfillment of creating a successful business are apparent. The sacrifices necessary to build and maintain a thriving enterprise require a special kind of person, typically an entrepreneur with limitless energy and dedication. One of the mixed blessings facing these people is the tendency to plow all their resources and profits back into the business. While often necessary to sustain growth, the practice frequently leads to the owner ignoring the need to set separate money aside for retirement. The value of the growing business may be perceived as insurance for retirement, but successfully liquidating a business in exchange for retirement funding is not guaranteed. My dentist who was almost forced out of business because of property ownership issues is a perfect example.

I work with my self-employed clients to get them to create a discrete investment account outside of their business to help ensure money will be there for their retirement, regardless of what happens to their business. So many factors can imperil a plan that relies on the value of a business to fund retirement. Competition can seize market share. Business conditions can change rapidly. Consider how technology has rendered so many seemingly invulnerable businesses and even industries obsolete. Canadian physicians who used to count on money from selling their practices can no longer do so. Like everyone else, business owners are subject to the fate of a disabling accident or illness. A lawsuit, legislation or partnership disagreement can propel a business into receivership.

Diversification is not just a term relating to investment asset allocation; it also applies to managing retirement risk for business owners.

A friend of mine, a very bright fellow, sold his manufacturing business for over a million dollars and retired. His hobby was restoring classic cars. As a result of not being able to control his passion for buying barn finds, he went through the entire amount he received for the business in less than five years. He and his wife were forced to sell their home and downsize. They receive OAS and CPP and, combined with the equity they had in their home, will probably be able to scrape by. But their lifestyle has changed dramatically and he can no longer afford to do the one thing he loved most. My hope is that he will change his habits and accept his lower standard of living.

My friend was fortunate to at least be able to liquidate his home in a reasonably strong real estate market. Suppose however that the market was in a downward spiral when he needed to sell it? That prospect may seem unlikely to Canadians who have enjoyed a thriving real estate environment for many years, but there's certainly no guarantee of a continuance. Just ask people who tried to sell their homes after 2009 in cities like Detroit or Cleveland, or retirees who tried to liquidate their condos in a Florida market flooded with unsold new properties. You don't ever want to put yourself in the position of relying on fortuitous timing to fund your retirement. We Canadians may well be nearing the end of the real estate rainbow. If you are living in Alberta, the rainbow has already disappeared due to the collapse of oil prices.

Those who are employed may believe they have security but even the largest, most successful companies suffer layoffs as a result of economic factors, poor management, competitive forces, tax issues, corporate takeovers, and the like. We previously discussed the heartbreaking experience of employees whose promised pensions were drastically reduced after retirement.

Interest Rates

The movement and direction of interest rates can be a significant factor, in particular for retirees reliant on fixed income investments. There is an argument from a demographics perspective that interest rates are likely to remain at lower levels for an extended period. One reason for this conclusion is the impact of the retiring baby boomer generation.

In their research paper, "Demographic Changes, Financial Markets, and the Economy,"[25] the authors conclude that, "...young adults, often in the process of starting a family, will rarely be major contributors to the quest for savings, investments, and capital accumulation. As they look past their own and their children's immediate needs to their eventual retirements, they begin to invest —first in stocks, then in bonds. As they slide into retirement, they begin to sell assets in order to buy goods and services that they no longer produce — either directly, through their own investments, or indirectly, through their pension benefits. They tend to liquidate their riskiest assets (stocks) before their less risky assets (bonds)."

The research also notes that, "Large populations of retirees (65+) seem to erode the performance of financial markets as well as economic growth." Obviously, diminishing economic growth tends to promote lower interest rates. And as people age, they tend to invest more conservatively, creating greater demand for bonds and other fixed-income investments, which in turn tends to suppress interest rates.

Inflation and Taxes

The impact of inflation and taxes adds to the complexity of planning. Inflation diminishes purchasing power over the years, and impedes the ability of retirees to maintain a desired lifestyle. It doesn't take much study to realize that planning for a potential retirement of two or three decades is not something individuals should tackle without professional help.

The rate of inflation is yet another unpredictable factor, subject to numerous influences. Escalating federal deficits may portend high future inflation. Demand for healthcare services by an aging population could push costs ever higher in coming years.

Individuals estimating their retirement income needs often overlook the potentially devastating impact of inflation. Bear markets cause some to abandon their long-term plans and shift assets into the perceived safety of GICs or similar bank products. That knee-jerk reaction to down markets can virtually guarantee they will not keep pace with inflation. A good advisor can help you stick to your plan during tough times and take acceptable investment risks to help ensure you won't outlive your money. Strategies to help offset the effects of inflation might include laddering bonds, annuities or specialized inflation-adjusted investments.

Taxes are another enemy of accumulating sufficient savings for retirement. I regularly hear people refer to the amount in their pension as their retirement nest egg. What they fail to consider is that the amount is going to be reduced by a significant percentage once the government siphons off its share in the form of taxes.

Miscalculations or failure to properly plan for taxes can dramatically alter the principal available to generate income during retirement. Strategies are available to reduce the impact of taxation but this is not an area for dilettantes. Advance planning and the specific knowledge necessary to implement tax strategy are the purview of financial professionals.

Withdrawal Rate

A common error made by retirees is excess portfolio withdraws. People regularly miscalculate their retirement income needs, then seek to correct the error by withdrawing additional money. If this continues, the portfolio's principal will be exhausted prematurely, eliminating its ability to provide income. Being in one's 70s or 80s is no time to begin looking for ways to accumulate additional principal.

Just because the markets have historically returned 8-10% annually doesn't mean you can withdraw that amount from your portfolio each year in retirement. As we have discussed, the markets are uncertain and irrational. You might get lucky and retire precisely as the markets begin a long upward ascent. You are just as likely to suffer losses in your first few years of retirement (sequence of returns risk) and be relegated to a much lower withdrawal rate than anticipated. The point is you can't predict whether the markets will deliver historical rates of return or how long you will be retired and need money, so you must protect your investment principal by accepting a realistic rate of withdrawal and being disciplined. You may have to accept lifestyle adjustments. The calculations can be complex and should be determined with a competent advisor.

Team Approach

I believe clients receive great value from a team advisory approach. Our clients who formerly worked with bank advisors complained about going through automated systems. When they did reach a live person, they frequently had to explain their circumstances all over again because service center turnover meant they rarely talked to the same person from year to year.

The team approach fosters continuity and familiarity with clients. Everyone in our office knows the circumstances of each of our clients, so when someone calls in, it doesn't matter who answers the phone, our client is recognized. We also try to make sure our staff has complementary competencies, whether client relations, analytics, research or other proficiencies. That's not possible in one-man shops or in banks or brokerages where there is constant employee turnover.

Having a team of dedicated personnel also allows us to react quickly in emergency situations so all our clients are kept in the information loop.

The market downturn of 2008 and early 2009 was a classic panic time for many investors. Those with highly speculative investments had good reason to be terrified but many people with solid investments also suffered anxiety and made rash decisions based on fear.

We spent hundreds of hours on the phone with our clients during this period. We called all of our clients to remind them that they held quality investments that would recover and that they had no reason to panic or make impulsive decisions. We wanted them to know that we were available at any time to answer questions and discuss their financial concerns. Additionally, we held a series of seminars for clients where we invited a panel of experts to discuss the markets and field questions. The combination of ongoing personal contact and seminars helped reassure our clients and got them through a particularly difficult time. When we talk about the value an experienced advisory team brings to the table, having financial professionals who have guided others through multiple market cycles can be invaluable in helping clients avoid making mistakes resulting from emotionally driven investment decisions.

Chapter 9

Strategies for a Successful Retirement

The question isn't at what age I want to retire; it's at what income.

≈ *George Foreman*

The concept of retirement has changed dramatically in recent decades. What was once regarded as a short interval of post-working years has commonly become an extended 20-30 year time period. While opening numerous opportunities for retirees, longer retirement also presents some serious financial challenges. Simply put, the longer you live, the more money you will need.

The likelihood of an extended retirement emphasizes the need for comprehensive planning and investment strategies. While each individual's lifestyle preferences and financial circumstances factor into the equation, plummeting into retirement without a roadmap makes no sense.

Retirement Plan or Retirement Estimate?

We offer our clients a variety of retirement plans, ranging from those that meet basic needs to highly sophisticated strategies for those with more complex requirements. However, not everyone requires a formal retirement plan; some people simply need a detailed retirement estimate that lets them know they will be able to maintain a comfortable lifestyle in their later years.

A retirement estimate covers the essential considerations of advance planning. When do you plan to retire? How much have you set aside for retirement? How much can you realistically save between now and retirement? Are you willing to make lifestyle changes now to help meet your retirement needs? Assuming inflation, how much purchasing power will you need in retirement to maintain your current lifestyle? What are your options if you don't have enough time to save what you need for retirement?

Here's a sobering thought: Given the dramatic increase in life expectancy, the number of years you spend in retirement may equal or even exceed the number of years you spent working. Health or economic factors may prevent you from earning additional income while retired. Given that uncertainty, you must ensure that your investments can generate sufficient income to provide for your basic needs, protect your purchasing power and cover emergencies.

A rule of thumb has been that retirees will need 65% to 70% of their pre-retirement income. While individual situations vary, I believe most people will require more — rather than less — in retirement. In addition to longevity, the cost of private healthcare and long term care tend to elevate financial needs.

An example of this occurred the other day when I was speaking to a client about a financial matter. She mentioned she was having severe pains and was told she would have to wait for a month to see a specialist. She couldn't wait because of the intense pain and so had to go to a private clinic. It cost her over $10,000 just for the necessary tests to get a diagnosis. I think this kind of event will become more common in the future because of the strain baby boomers will be putting on the medical system. Retirement planning should include a provision for out of pocket costs for private healthcare because it can happen to anyone.

You cannot rely on government programs to cover your retirement needs. The Canada pension Plan (CPP) is designed to pay approximately 25% of your average earnings. Relying on that would mean a drastic reduction in your quality of life. Old Age Security (OAS) is a safety net designed to provide basic income but benefits are reduced (clawed back) for individuals whose net income exceeds

$72,809. In 2016, for each $1 of income above this limit, the OAS pension is reduced by $0.15.

You must take responsibility for your retirement as it will largely be determined by your own efforts. The key is to create a realistic plan and commit to it. Above all, you must avoid procrastinating.

> *Preparation for retirement should begin not later than one's teens. A life that is empty of purpose until 65 will not suddenly become filled on retirement.*
>
> ≈ *Arthur E Morgan*

Sources of Income

Government Pension Benefits (CPP and OAS) were previously discussed in the chapter on *Financial Obstacles*. In review, CPP is a contributory program that pays income to contributors and family members in the event of retirement, disability or death. The amount of the CPP pension depends on the contributions made during your working years. For 2016, the maximum pension is approximately $1092 per month. CPP benefits are adjusted annually based on the Consumer Price Index and are included in total income for tax purposes. Benefits are designed to start at age 65 but you may choose to begin receiving them earlier or later.

There are numerous considerations regarding when to start taking benefits. To request an article discussing this topic, email me at eric.muir@raymondjames.ca or phone 604.451.3100.

The OAS benefit is for anyone age 65 or older who has been a Canadian citizen or resident for at least 10 years. The maximum OAS pension benefit for 2016 is $570 per month and is taxable income.

Registered Pension Plans (RPP) are retirement programs sponsored by employers. Both employers and employees can make pre-tax contributions to these plans, subject to government regulations.

Defined benefit plans provide a specific pension benefit, based on an employee's income and length of employment. The employer is responsible for making contributions and investing them to ensure participants will receive the specified retirement income benefit.

Defined contribution (or money purchase) plans have no income guarantees. Participants make contributions, typically a percentage of their earnings. Employers have the option of matching a part of employee contributions. At retirement, the accumulated funds are typically used to purchase an annuity that pays monthly income for the life of the participant.

Deferred Profit Sharing Plans (DPSP) allow employers to designate a percentage of the firm's profits as a reward for employees.

The annual contribution limits for 2016 are $25,370 for a defined contribution RPP and half that for a DPSP. The 2015 maximum pension benefit for a defined benefit RPP (per year of service) is $2,890.

RRSP

A Registered Retirement Savings Plan (RRSP) allows you to defer tax on money to be used for retirement. RRSP contribution limits are based on your earned income[26] and are tax deductible at the time of deposit, up to a ceiling amount. Funds grow tax-deferred until withdrawn, which allows your money to compound more rapidly than if you had to pay income tax on each year's growth.

Anyone 71 or younger with earned income[27] can contribute 18 percent of their earned income for the previous year (plus any unused contributions) up to the maximum annual contribution limit for the year, reduced by any contributions to an RPP. Contributions can be made anytime during the year and up to 60 days into the following year. Individuals must begin taking withdrawals no later than the end of the year they turn 72.

In the case of a special event that does not qualify as earned income; an individual may be able to contribute larger amounts to an RRSP. Let's assume Joe has never contributed into an RRSP. At age 70 and having been retired for five years, he sells a property, triggering a taxable capital gain of $200,000. Since he has never contributed, he has room to put that $200,000 into an RRSP to offset the capital gain, even though he might not have any earned income for the year.

The great RRSP advantage

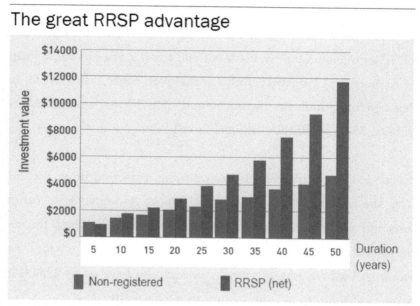

Hypothesis: Growth of an annual $1,000 investment in an RRSP and a non-registered vehicle. Based on a 6% annual return, with a 40% marginal tax rate.

SOURCE: THE MUIR INVESTMENT TEAM

A self-directed RRSP allows you to choose the products and asset mix in your RRSP investment portfolio, subject to eligibility. As the owner of a self-directed RRSP, you are responsible for ensuring that the investments meet the legal requirements set by the Canada Revenue Agency. Not meeting this standard results in the loss of the income tax deduction.

RRSPs are established under the *Income Tax Act* and are not pensions. Therefore, you can withdraw money from an RRSP at any time provided you pay the tax on the withdrawal, whether investment, interest or dividend income. An RRSP must be converted by the end of the year in which you turn 71. Since money within an RRSP has not been taxed, withdrawals are taxable as income. There are three RRSP conversion options: Cash out and pay the taxes in a lump sum — a horrifying prospect from a tax perspective, convert to an Registered Retirement Income Fund (RRIF) or convert to an annuity. More about these options shortly.

If your RRSP contribution is less than the deduction limit, you can carry the unused "deduction room" forward indefinitely to future years and add it to the calculation of those deduction limits. Income tax deductions can also be carried forward, which provides tax planning flexibility. At any time, you may also have up to $2,000 in excess contributions in your account without penalty.

An element of planning many people are unaware of is the Pension Income Tax Credit. It enables Canadians to deduct a tax credit equal to the lesser of their pension income or $2,000. Individuals age 65 without a Canadian Pension Plan can transfer $12,000 from their RRSP to an RRIF and take out $2,000 per year from ages 65 through 71. This allows them to get $2,000 per year out of their RRSP tax-free for six years. Alternately, individuals can open a RRIF and each year transfer $2,000 from their RRSP into the RRIF, then pay it out to themselves tax-free.

I was discussing the pension income deduction with a prospective client, age 70, whose current advisor neglected to recommend the strategy to him. The tax savings would have provided him with an additional $5,400 he could have put in his pocket instead of donating it to the government. The saving also applied to his wife, as she is approaching age 70 and has not been transferring the $2,000 per year from her RRSP to an RRIF either. Now this couple is worth several million so the tax savings are not monumental, but it was just that someone he trusted for reliable financial counsel missed a good opportunity to save some taxes. It also made him think what else he might not know about that was costing him money. When we talk about an advisor providing value, most people think about investment returns. But there are other areas that collectively can be just as important as a point or two on their portfolio's rate of return. As the saying goes, "it's not what you make but what you keep."

RRSP owners buying their first home or taking post-secondary education can take up to $25,000 out of their RRSP prior to retirement age without penalty provided the required repayments are made.

You and your spouse can each have an RRSP. You are allowed to allocate all or a portion of your contributions to either account. Contributions to your spouse's account count against your contribution limit and you receive the tax deduction, but your spouse can still make a full contribution to his or her account.

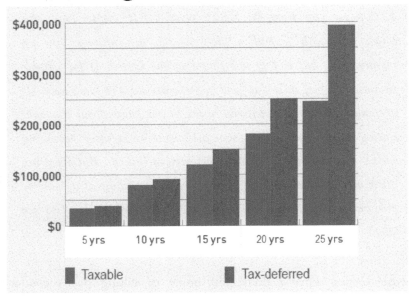

Annual contribution:	$5,000
Combined income tax bracket:	40.0%
Tax-deferred return:	8.0%
Taxable return:	4.8%

Tax-deferred growth

Assumes contribution made at beginning of each year and compounded annually. Not representative of the performance of any specific investment.

SOURCE: THE MUIR INVESTMENT TEAM

The strategy allows working couples with similar incomes to literally double their tax deductions. If one spouse has significantly lower income, the income-balancing strategy can meaningfully lower the amount of tax due upon withdrawal. It also allows someone with a younger spouse to continue making contributions after reaching age

71 up until the end of the year the younger spouse reaches age 71. If a spouse is designated as beneficiary of an RRSP (or RPP), the account can be transferred to the surviving spouse and treated as if it were that spouse's account. Income splitting is not subject to subsequent tax rule changes if the strategy is implemented at the time of contribution versus the time of withdrawal.

RRIF

A Registered Retirement Income Fund (RRIF) is a tax-deferred retirement plan designed to generate income from contributions accumulated in an RRSP. While RRSPs are designed to amass funds, RRIFs are designed to pay funds out. The monies remaining in a RRIF remain tax sheltered. An RRIF provides the same investment flexibility as an RRSP. Anything that can be held in an RRSP can be held in an RRIF so the investment mix can be tailored to your specific needs. An RRIF can be established at any time, regardless of age. Typically, they are set up at retirement or before the end of the year a person reaches age 71.

There are no *maximum* limits on RRIF withdrawals. You can withdraw the entire value of the RRIF at any time. However, withdrawals are fully taxed in the year of withdrawal. There are *minimum* withdrawal requirements that must be taken every year. The amount, which varies by age, is prescribed by the *Income Tax Act* and is equal to a percentage of the fair market value of the RRIF assets on December 31st each year.

An alternative to converting an RRSP to an RRIF is to convert the RRSP to an annuity. This option sometimes appeals to individuals wary of stock market risk. However, annuity payouts are based on interest rates and with current rates extremely low, the annuity is not an option I would recommend. If you convert to an RRIF, the option of annuitizing the RRIF is available to you at any time in the future, perhaps when interest rates are higher. However, once you annuitize, you cannot convert back to an RRIF.

Currently, minimum percentage to be withdrawn ranges from 5.28% at age 71 to 20% at age 95 and older. So for example, if your RRIF is valued at one million dollars when you are age 72, your minimum withdrawal requirement for that calendar year will be $54,000 or 5.40% of the value of your RRIF. The withdrawal factor for those younger than age 71 is determined by the formula 1/(90-age). If you are 65 or older, you can split RRIF income with your spouse.

Existing and New RRIF Factors

Age (at start of year)	Existing Factor (%)	New Factor (%)
71	7.38	5.28
72	7.48	5.40
73	7.59	5.53
74	7.71	5.67
75	7.85	5.82
76	7.99	5.98
77	8.15	6.17
78	8.33	6.36
79	8.53	6.58
80	8.75	6.82
81	8.99	7.08
82	9.27	7.38
83	9.58	7.71
84	9.93	8.08
85	10.33	8.51
86	10.79	8.99
87	11.33	9.55
88	11.96	10.21
89	12.71	10.99
90	13.62	11.92
91	14.73	13.06
92	16.12	14.49
93	17.92	16.34
94	20.00	18.79
95 +	20.00	20.00

SOURCE: CANADA REVENUE AGENCY

TFSA

Canadian residents who have reached the age of majority (18 or 19 years, depending on the province) and with a valid Canadian social insurance number can open a Tax-Free Savings Account (TFSA) to set money aside during their lifetime. The contribution limit for 2016 is $5,500 and is expected to remain at that level indefinitely. Subject to certain exceptions, a TFSA is generally permitted to hold the same types of investments as an RRSP or investment account.

The TFSA is a registered savings account in which interest, dividends, capital gains and other investment income is earned tax-free. The income and capital can be withdrawn tax-free. Unlike an RRSP, you can withdraw money from a TFSA at any time without paying tax. However, withdrawals can affect your ability to contribute more to your TFSA in the same year. If, for example, you have made your full contribution to the allowable maximum of $46,500 and you remove money, you cannot redeposit that money back into your TFSA in the same year. You must wait until the following year.

Unlike an RRSP, you do not receive a tax deduction for contributions to a TFSA. However, you do not have to include any income, losses or gains from investments held within a TFSA, or amounts withdrawn from it in your income for tax purposes. Amounts withdrawn from a TFSA will also not be included in determining your eligibility for income-tested benefits or credits, such as the medical or age credit or OAS clawback.

If you don't contribute to your TFSA in one year, the amount can be carried forward indefinitely to future years. Any amounts withdrawn from a TFSA can also be re-contributed without impacting your contribution room. Interest on money borrowed to invest in a TFSA is not deductible.

A TFSA is generally permitted to hold similar investments as an RRSP or investment account, including cash, mutual funds, ETFs, publicly traded securities, GICs, bonds, and certain shares of small business corporations.

You can contribute to your spouse's TFSA as well as your own without any negative tax consequences. This could allow you to reduce your family's total tax bill.

Working After Retirement

Financial flexibility in retirement enables you to choose whether to continue working on your own terms. You may decide to pursue entrepreneurial ambitions or give back to your community or other worthy causes.

Income from continued work can play an important role in maintaining financial security in retirement. However, many retirees say the nonfinancial benefits of working are even more important. Working retirees also say that staying physically active, maintaining social connections, and having a strong sense of self-worth are more important reasons to work than the money

Financial flexibility is the difference between working to maintain a lifestyle or to fulfill personal interests, and working to pay for basic necessities. It's being able to choose enjoyable, rewarding work or volunteering, or having to choose based on how much a job pays.

Knowledge for a Successful Retirement

Here are some important factors to remember in pursuing a successful retirement:

➤ Procrastination may pose the greatest threat to a satisfactory retirement. Set realistic goals and start saving early.

➤ A successful retirement strategy should not rely primarily on investment performance. It should be based on a realistic retirement estimate and a commitment to the plan.

➤ Take responsibility for understanding financial fundamentals. Spend the time to learn about investments, their risks and tax consequences.

➤ Ignore the clamor from the media and others who spread misinformation. When seemingly everyone is convinced that "this time is different," rely on your plan and the counsel of someone who has been through it all before to remind you to keep your bearings and avoid overreaction to the noise.

➢ Inflation, interest rate and pension risk all represent threats to a successful retirement. Make sure these and other financial obstacles are factored into your retirement plan.

➢ Longevity, health and employment issues can imperil your retirement. Provide for these contingencies in your plan.

➢ Review your plan, asset allocation, personal circumstances, and goals each year.

➢ The markets are rarely as good or bad as they appear. Personal biases have a significant impact on investment performance. Be aware of common predispositions to project recent events into the future, fixate on past events, be over weighted in domestic securities, and emotional decision-making.

➢ Find an advisor whose experience includes guiding clients through difficult economic times — a trustworthy financial partner with the confidence to disagree with you when you are about to make a mistake.

ERIC MUIR

As in all successful ventures, the foundation of a good retirement is planning.

≈ Earl Nightingale

Chapter 10

Tax Considerations

In levying taxes and in shearing sheep it is well to stop when you get down to the skin.

≈ *Austin O'Malley*

Tax considerations are an integral part of retirement planning. You need to be aware of the impact of taxes on your investments during your working years, the limited span of time you have to accumulate sufficient funds for a comfortable retirement.

You must be smart about how you invest your money. The more money you can keep in your portfolio versus paying it out in taxes, the better it is because it allows you to accumulate retirement funds faster. If you hold investments outside of a Registered Retirement Savings Plan (RRSP) or Tax-Free Savings Account (TFSA), you have to know what investments are better than others for that type of account.

You must acquire a good understanding about which investments are better suited to help you keep more of your money and accelerate your retirement savings. You must be aware of how income from various investments — such as capital gains, dividends and GIC income — are treated from a tax perspective. As an example, people in the top tax bracket living in British Columbia in 2016 pay 47.7% personal income tax on their salary and interest income. They pay significantly less, however, on income from eligible dividends (31.30%) and capital gains (23.85%).

Each of the three types of investment income is taxed at a different marginal rate, affecting the amount you keep after taxes. The following graphic depicts the difference.

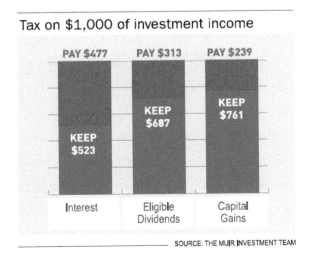

Tax on $1,000 of investment income

SOURCE: THE MUIR INVESTMENT TEAM

As you can see, if you have income from a savings account or guaranteed income certificate (GIC), you would keep just $5,230 of every $10,000 of investment income after taxes. On the other hand, you would keep $6,870 of each $10,000 of investment income from eligible dividends and $7,615 of each $10,000 of investment income from capital gains. That's a huge disparity, not only how much money you keep, but also how much more investment principle you retain to continue earning more investment income each year.

The variety of available investments and where each fits best into the tax equation can be confusing. The following graphic displays the various investments and the type of account potentially best suited for each.

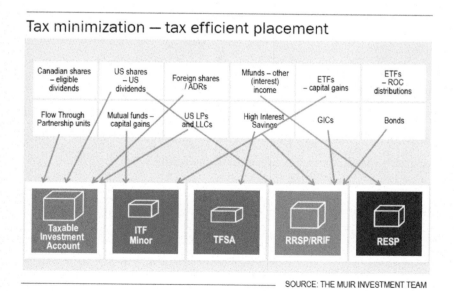

Tax minimization — tax efficient placement

SOURCE: THE MUIR INVESTMENT TEAM

With an eye towards tax efficiency, I typically suggest clients maximize their RRSP and apply any tax refunds towards paying down their mortgage, or, lacking a mortgage, putting the refund into their TFSA. The exception would be for someone in the lowest tax bracket, that is, earning less than $45,282, who might do better putting the money into a TFSA than an RRSP. Those who intend to send their children to college should be putting money into a Registered Education Savings Plan (RESP) before they do a TFSA because the government provides up to $500 each year on a $2,500 annual contribution. That's represents a 20% investment gain that's too good to pass up for parents. In British Columbia, it gets even better for parents who open a RESP after their child's 6th and before the 9th birthday: The BC Training and Education Savings Program (BCTESP) will pay $1,200 to each child's RESP without any contributions required by the parents!

For a tax efficient investment outside of tax-advantaged accounts (RRSP, TFSA and RESP), corporate class mutual funds can be useful as they convert interest income into eligible dividends or capital gains income, which is, of course, taxed at a much lower rate. There are also bond funds that achieve the same result.

Regarding tax considerations for retirement, if you are considering taking your Canada Pension Plan early, there are a number of calculations that come into play, including life expectancy and the funding required for lifestyle and investment needs. Given the complexity of the calculations, it's probably best to consult a financial advisor regarding when to start taking benefits. This is one area you should not tackle by yourself.

If you and your spouse both work and are in different tax brackets, you should consider splitting income. Our Canadian tax system allows you to shift income from a high tax income earner to family members in lower tax brackets in order to reduce overall family tax liability.

Income splitting

No income splitting	Jack	Jill	Totals
Income	$150,000	$20,000	$170,000
Taxes	$45,527	$1,491	$47,018

Income splitting	Jack	Jill	Totals
Income	$120,000	$50,000	$170,000
Taxes	$32,906	$8,610	$41,516

Taxes saved by splitting income	$5,502

SOURCE: THE MUIR INVESTMENT TEAM

Here are a few examples of simple income splitting strategies:

> Give money to your spouse and children over age 18 so they can maximize their TFSA contributions and earn tax-free income.

➢ Open an In Trust for Minor account (ITFM) for each of your children using investments that generate capital gains income exclusively.

➢ Contribute to a spousal RRSP, especially if that spouse plans to retire many years after the contributor or if the spouse will be in a much lower tax bracket at retirement.

➢ Maintain separate accounts for each spouse. The higher income spouse pays household expenses so the lower income spouse can invest his or her earnings. This strategy provides proof in case of a tax audit.

➢ Taxpayers 65 and older can split pension plan payments, RRIF payments, deferred profit share payments, and regular annuities.

Chapter 11

Your Estate

*Some taxpayers close their eyes, some stop their ears, some
shut their mouths, but all pay through the nose.*

≈ Evan Esar

Estate planning is an area of your financial life that should never be
neglected. It's a complex puzzle comprised of many pieces that you
should not try to solve without professional help.

People are often amazed to discover how much wealth they have
accumulated when we create an inventory of their assets. Proper
planning can ensure the disposition of those assets is aligned with
your wishes, but the devil is in the details.

How often do we hear horror stories about affluent individuals or
celebrities whose fortunes were thrown into legal chaos after their

deaths because of mistakes, outdated documents, fundamental omissions or procrastination? It's shocking to learn that individuals with so much to lose failed to take advantage of readily available estate planning strategies.

Warren Burger, a lawyer who rose to become Chief Justice of the United States Supreme Court, drafted his own will for reasons that remain a mystery today. The 172-word document resulted in his $1.8 million estate going into probate court and his family having to pay $450,000 in estate taxes that could have been avoided.[28]

When she died in 2007, hotel tycoon Leona Helmsley's will left most of her $5 billion estate to charity, created a $12 million trust for her Maltese dog, Trouble, and completely cut out two of her four grandchildren. The two stiffed grandkids sued her estate, claiming she wasn't mentally fit to create her will and trust. The case settled, with the dog getting $2 million and the two grandkids sharing $6 million plus legal fees.[29]

Pablo Picasso died in 1973 at the age of 91, leaving behind a fortune in assets that included artwork, five homes, cash, gold and bonds. Because Picasso died intestate and left no will, it took 6 years to settle his estate at a cost of $30 million. His assets were eventually divided up among six heirs.[30]

TV commentator Andy Rooney died at age 90 with an estate worth $9 million but without an estate plan. His family was forced to pay taxes of $2.3 million.

The family of Miami Dolphin's owner Joe Robbie was forced to sell the franchise to pay an estate tax bill estimated at $47 million.

The children of Jackie Kennedy Onassis were forced to sell many of their mother's cherished assets to raise an additional $5 million to pay an estate tax bill. The world may have been enamored with the Sotheby's auction but it was emotionally trying for John and Caroline Kennedy.

By definition, estate planning is a methodical process of organizing and managing your affairs designed to help you meet your goals. The plan should be tailored to your specific financial and personal circumstances. Typical estate planning elements include wills, powers of attorneys, representation agreements, joint tenancy and trusts. Generally, several advisors — financial planner, investment manager, estate planning attorney and accountant — should be included in the process.

A comprehensive estate plan should give you peace of mind while you are living by providing advance instructions — both financial and healthcare — in case of your incapacity. It should also help you avoid having the court appoint a committee to oversee your care and finances.

When you die, your estate plan should determine who will manage your affairs; who will get what; and how and when they will get it. It should minimize taxes, reduce or eliminate probate costs, avoid publicity if desired and again, provide serenity. If you have underage children, the plan should appoint a guardian. It should provide protection from a government appointed trustee or committee taking control over your assets in case of extreme disability or death. In addition to dictating who will receive what and when after your death, it should protect your estate and your loved ones in case of severe disability.

Here's a sobering statistic: 25% to 40% of the population will become mentally incapacitated at some time in their lifetime.[31] What would happen if you were alive but mentally incapacitated? Who would make your decisions and control your assets?

If you have not designated a power of attorney, the Provincial Government may assume control of your affairs. The Public Guardian and Trustee (PGT) has wide ranging powers to manage your personal and financial affairs. Not only would you lose control but at a significant cost. Your family may be powerless to do anything for you with the PGT's approval.

An alternative to a PGT is a Committeeship, a person appointed by the BC Supreme Court to make personal, medical, legal and financial decisions for you because you are unable to make them. The cost runs from $5,000 to $7,000 or more if contested.

A client awoke one Saturday morning to discover her husband had suffered a massive heart attack during the night. By the time the ambulance arrived, his brain had suffered irreparable damage. He was 54 years old, fit and with no history of heart problems. Eight years later, he remains hospitalized with no hope of recovery. His wife did not have an enduring power of attorney so a committeeship took over his affairs. She has suffered both emotional and financial distress as a result.

Powers of Attorneys

Three documents are necessary to allow you to appoint someone to take care of things should you become mentally incapable: an enduring power of attorney, a representation agreement and advance directives.

A power of attorney (POA) document permits someone you designate (the attorney) the right to handle some or all of your legal and financial affairs while you are alive. The POA is in effect only when you are mentally incapable and immediately ends when you become mentally capable. It is typically used for short-term assistance, such as during an illness or injury recovery. You are free to revoke a POA at any time but you must provide notice.

An enduring power of attorney (EPA) is generally for the longer term as it typically takes effect when you are mentally incapable, although you can create an EPA to take effect when you are capable as well as when you are not.

Both the POA and EPA documents can cover your legal and financial affairs but neither can cover health or personal care matters. Both become invalid when a donor dies and cannot be used to bequeath property upon the death of the donor.

There is also a bank power of attorney, which allows the person you designate to deal with your financial affairs at a specific institution, such as managing your bank accounts.[32]

The EPA offers the advantages of a simple form, inexpensive cost and the assurance of having a background of judicial interpretation. The disadvantages include being limited to legal and financial matters and not allowing the appointment of alternative attorneys (designated persons). There have been instances of abuse of power by naïve or fraudulent attorneys.

Representation Agreements

A representation Agreement (RA) is a legal document authorizing someone you designate to assist you or act in your behalf for health and personal care matters. It can also cover legal matters. It permits the appointment of both separate and alternative representatives for different or specific functions. In accepting, a representative has a fiduciary duty, which encompasses acting with honesty and in good faith on behalf of the donor, keeping accurate accounts and consulting with the donor on decisions when practical.

The donor may also designate a monitor, someone to provide a second opinion and provide oversight to the representative.

There are disadvantages to a RA. It's a more complex document than a POA; its execution requirements are more complex and time consuming than a POA; it's more expensive than an EPA; it's not acknowledged in most other jurisdictions; and it may be unfamiliar to many financial institutions.

Advance Directives

Part of creating an advance care plan is an advance directive, instructions for health and personal care given to your healthcare provider. This might include directives about whether you want life supporting or life prolonging medical interventions. Advance directives are binding on both representatives and healthcare providers.

Assets

Your estate is different before and after your death. How you own your assets determines whether they become part of your estate when you die.

At death, your estate is comprised of both your tangible and intangible assets. All your tangible assets, including your home, real estate and automobiles, jewelry, precious metals and personal possessions, become part of your estate —provided they are not owned jointly. Your intangible assets, including bank accounts, deposits, stocks, bonds, funds and life insurance payable to the estate also become part of your estate, if owned solely by you as opposed to being owned jointly. Other intangibles, such as your RRSP, RRIF and deferred annuities, also become part of your estate if they have no designated beneficiary.

After death, some of your assets can avoid probate by using one of several strategies, including joint ownership, designating beneficiaries, assured annuities or establishing trusts. Probate can be a lengthy process that is costly and increases taxes.

So if a married couple owns an asset jointly, when one dies, the property moves into the estate of the surviving spouse, provided joint ownership is with rights of survivorship. Joint tenancy can provide a sense of family unity and security. Property is passed by "right of survivorship" so the surviving joint tenant does not suffer the loss of the asset. It also reduces the likelihood of claims under the Wills Estates and Succession Act (WESA).

As with any strategy, there are potential disadvantages to joint tenancy. As an individual, you do not have sole control of the asset(s); you cannot specify any limitations or restrictions on the surviving owner; your interest — and those of your heirs — ceases when you die; assets may be subject to the creditors of the joint tenant; and the potential for complex income tax issues exists.

While assets placed in joint tenancy avoid probate, problems can arise when couples include their children on the title.

A couple put their two children on title for their assets in joint tenancy with right to survivor on their property. Their rationale was that since the kids will eventually get everything anyway, now they don't have to worry about their property going through the will. But in doing so, the couple loses control of the property and they can't specify how those assets get divided between the two children. If either of the children gets into financial trouble, their creditors can make claims against the property, not an insignificant problem.

One family that included their son on joint tenancy title saw their retirement thrown into turmoil when he was involved in an automobile accident while driving intoxicated. The parent's assets subsequently came under siege from the lawyer for the family whose member was killed in the accident. It's also not at all uncommon for the good intentions of the parents to result in their children fighting over the dispersion of their parent's assets. What was intended to provide security for children ends up creating anger and infighting between them.

Some other instances of unintended consequences arising from the use (or misuse) of joint tenancy:

A couple's will designated their four children as equal beneficiaries. The estate's principal asset — their home — was placed in joint tenancy with eldest child, who decided to keep the house for himself. Subsequent litigation by his siblings to claim a piece of the property was successful but took several years and cost thousands of dollars. The ultimate result was broken family relationships.

A mother places her daughter, the only child, on her property in joint tenancy. The daughter is sued for a poor business decision and a $700,000 judgment is registered against her half interest in her mother's home.

Parents transfer their cottage into joint tenancy with their children and are subsequently assessed a capital gain on the disposition of the interest transferred. This occurs because transferring title of an asset — even if money hasn't changed hands — generally results in the asset deemed being sold at fair market value, triggering capital gains tax.

Parents transfer their long-held family home into joint tenancy with their son. The parents later decide they wish to sell the property to downsize, travel and enjoy their retirement. The son wants to hold on the home and refuses to sell. A contested application under the Partition and Sale of Property Act is brought and eventually the property is sold but it eats up significant legal fees and the parents and their son no longer speak to each other.

An older man remarries and places his largest asset (his home) into joint tenancy with his new wife. When he dies, the asset passes to the new wife, depriving the children from his first marriage of any participation in the home and with no way to challenge the will.

Trusts

There are a number of different types of trusts and it's rather easy for people to get confused about the various applications. Three of the most common types of trust are testamentary, alter ego and joint spousal

A <u>testamentary trust</u> goes into effect upon an individual's death and is typically used when someone wants to leave assets to a beneficiary, but doesn't want the beneficiary to receive those assets until a specified time. Testamentary trusts are irrevocable. For example, a parent might create a testamentary trust to leave assets to a minor child so that the child would not receive the assets until he or she became an adult and could manage them responsibly. A trustee would manage the testamentary trust's assets until the beneficiary receives control of them.[33]

A testamentary trust can be useful in situations where you're concerned about the beneficiary's ability to manage the money you're giving them in your will.

A client of mine died and left his money to his three children. Unfortunately, one of the sons had a drug issue so the father did not want to leave him a lump sum of money. He formed a testamentary trust that was embedded in his will and took effect upon his death. It directed that the troubled son would get $24,000 a year plus a lump sum of $20,000 every two years for the rest of his life or for however long the money lasted. His brother was designated trustee of the testamentary trust so the son can't go off and blow the whole wad on drugs.

Both <u>alter ego trusts</u> and <u>joint spousal trusts</u> are *inter vivos* trusts, meaning they are created during the life of the owner or *settlor*, the term for someone who has established a trust. An alter ego trust is set up for the benefit of one individual; the joint spousal trust is created for a couple.

Both types of trusts avoid triggering deemed disposition[34] and capital gains. The individual settlor is the only beneficiary of an alter ego trust whereas only the spouses may be beneficiary of a joint spousal trust.

A designated trustee(s) becomes the legal owner of the assets in the trust, while the settlor(s) remains entitled to the income and capital, and is responsible for any income taxes arising out of the holdings.[35]

These trusts can be advantageous if you are age 65 or older, wish to continue receiving the income from the trust until you (or you and your partner) die and you want the beneficiary to have quick access to the assets upon your death. The assets held in either trust are not included in your estate and so are not subject to probate. As such, the trustee can distribute the trust assets to the beneficiaries immediately upon the settlor's death.

We created an alter ego trust for my mother, who is 89. The trust owns her home and all her investments. When she dies, she won't have an estate; her alter ego trust owns everything. It's an alternative way of dealing with an estate by taking all her assets out of her estate and putting them into the trust. The beneficiaries remain the same as they would be in a will but we will save roughly $20,000 in probate fees. Also, nobody can contest it. If somebody feels like they aren't getting their fair share, they can contest the will and create havoc. With an alter ego or joint spousal trust, no one can contest it.

A caveat: Generally speaking, I don't suggest creating these types of trusts until later in life. The downside is that you must file separate tax returns for the trusts every year, which typically costs a few hundred dollars. If you created the trust and then lived for another thirty years, the tax filing costs will eat into the savings.

With a joint spousal trust, as long as one of the two spouses is alive, only they can be capital or income beneficiaries of the trust. When the last of the two spouses die, what remains can be distributed to the residual beneficiaries, typically the children. As long as one of the spouses is alive, the children cannot receive income or capital out of the trust.

In my experience, most seniors are unaware of the fact that these types of trusts offer an appealing alternative. But estate planning is not the easiest topic to talk about, which is perhaps why so few advisors I know spend much time discussing estate planning with their clients. As an advisor, you need expertise in this area if you are going to help your clients with estate and tax issues. You have to devote time to understand the topic in order to be able to do your clients some good. It's a hugely problematic issue for anyone with significant assets.

I have been conducting estate planning seminars for my clients for nearly twenty years. I have a close relationship with an experienced estate planning lawyer who keeps me updated on changes in regulations and tax laws and conducts workshops with me. New legislation, such as WESA (2014), illustrates the need to have someone with extensive knowledge of estate issues constantly monitoring the changes on your team.

A note from Stephen Miller, the estate planning attorney who I regularly work with:

In December, I met with a client on a Thursday afternoon regarding his testamentary will. The client died on the following Sunday before the will could be completed.

As you are probably aware, under the old legislation (Estate Administration Act and Wills Act) a person's testamentary intentions could only be in the form of a will validly created in accordance with the Wills Act. In instances where clients died prior to signing their wills or signed them without witnesses, the will simply could not be probated and relied upon regardless of what extrinsic evidence (evidence of lawyers, family, etc.) could be presented that, in fact, the deceased wanted to distribute their estate a particular way.

WESA changed this and permits an application requesting the court to acknowledge the extrinsic evidence as being the deceased's testamentary intention and admitting it to probate as if it were a will.

Relying on the new section of WESA, I applied to have my notes from the Thursday meeting admitted as the deceased's testamentary intention and presented a draft will that I prepared but the deceased never had a chance to review. On the strength of the new law and the thoroughness of my notes, the Court has ordered that the draft will prepared from my notes be treated as a valid will, thus avoiding an intestacy.

As you can see, the value of having competent professional representation cannot be overemphasized.

Shrinkage

Estates can shrink for several reasons. Federal and Provincial taxes can erode an estate.

When academy award winning actor Philip Seymour Hoffman died from drug intoxication in 2014, he left an estate worth an estimated $35 million. After the $5.34 million estate tax exemption, the balance of his estate — roughly $30 million — was taxed at 40%. In addition, his will was written in 2004 after the birth of his child with companion Mimi O'Donnell. He had two more children but never updated his will to include them, and because he and O'Donnell never married, her inheritance didn't qualify for the unlimited marital deduction under estate tax law in the U.S., *which meant the IRS would claim an additional $12 million from the estate. That's shrinkage!*

What's often referred to as the "hidden estate tax" is deemed disposition, which makes the assumption that simultaneous with your death, all your assets were sold at fair market value. The profits or capital gain of what was sold (what you sold everything for minus your costs) is what you get taxed on, even though you actually didn't sell anything.

It can be especially problematic with rental properties and similar investments where the property has been depreciated for accounting purposes to offset the rental income. If someone bought a rental property for $100,000 and owned it for thirty years, they've fictionally depreciated it down to zero. When they die, the property is worth $200,000. The first $100,000 in value is considered recaptured depreciation, which is taxable as ordinary income. The $100,000 gain in value is considered capital gain and taxed accordingly.

For estate tax purposes, RRSPs, RRIFs and LIFs are taxed as ordinary income of the deceased for the tax year of their death. The tax on an RRSP or RRIF can be deferred if the beneficiary is a spouse or common law partner, a dependent child or grandchild under the age of 18, or a mentally or physically dependent child or grandchild of any age.

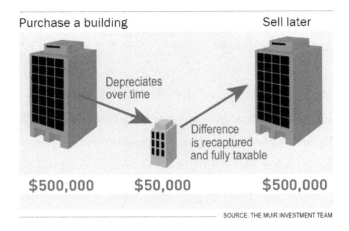

Purchase a building — Sell later

Depreciates over time

Difference is recaptured and fully taxable

$500,000 $50,000 $500,000

SOURCE: THE MUIR INVESTMENT TEAM

The RRSP or RRIF can be used to buy an annuity that pays regular income until the dependent child or grandchild turns 18. In the case of an impaired child or grandchild, a life annuity or fixed term annuity payable to age 90 can be purchased. Alternately, the RRSP or RRIF can be moved to an RRSP in the child's name.

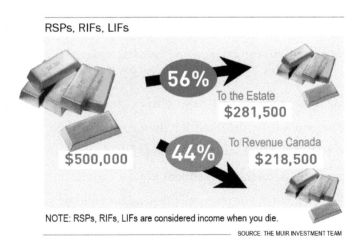

RSPs, RIFs, LIFs

56% To the Estate $281,500

$500,000   44%   To Revenue Canada $218,500

NOTE: RSPs, RIFs, LIFs are considered income when you die.

SOURCE: THE MUIR INVESTMENT TEAM

Other causes of estate shrinkage are transfer costs, including probate, administrative costs and professional fees for appraisers, lawyers and accountants. A tragedy resulting from shrinkage can occur if the estate doesn't have enough liquid assets to pay these obligations. The executor may be forced to sacrifice property or business interests at fire-sale prices. The result can be emotionally and financially devastating to the heirs.

Funding Estate Transfer Costs

One of the most cost-efficient methods of providing money for estate transfer costs is life insurance. For a couple, joint last to die insurance is less costly and can make sense as it is paid to offset the estate costs of the second spouse to die because that's when the insurance is needed. It's not needed when the first spouse dies because all of the estate gets transferred to the spouse tax free and deferred. It's when the last of the two die when the estate taxes are payable.

Life insurance proceeds are tax free, prevent having to sell investments to pay tax liabilities at an inopportune time, provide cash that bypasses wills and probate with a named beneficiary, and is creditor protected.

Giving Away Assets

Giving away assets while you are alive is a way to reduce current taxes and do something good for a charity or your heirs. You can give away any assets that have value.

Many people have misconceptions about giving assets to their children. You are allowed to give assets to your children but any appreciable assets other than your principal residence will trigger capital gains. For example, you can give your cottage to your children but be aware that you are required to pay the capital gains taxes on the appreciation of the property.

If you decide to give to charity in your will, giving appreciated assets can make sense. For example, if you have a stock portfolio that's appreciated significantly, gift the portfolio instead of gifting cash because your estate won't have to pay capital gains tax and also gets the tax receipt for the value of what you gave. There are strategies to gift constructively.

Sometimes, it's difficult for people to see any tangible benefit to planning and paying for events they may not wish to discuss or may not believe will eventually happen. But being able to save estate taxes, avoid probate and lessen the chances for family discord provides very real value. The serenity of knowing your spouse and heirs will not be forced to liquidate assets to pay taxes in a stressful environment is, in itself, ample justification for the cost. The ultimate benefit may be how good you will feel about how much easier everything will be when your time inevitably arrives.

The art of taxation consists in so plucking the goose as to obtain the largest amount of feathers with the least possible amount of squawking.

≈ *Jean Baptiste Cobert, "The Theory and Practice of Taxation."*

Epilogue

Economics is all about consumption. People either spend money now or they use financial instruments — like bonds, stocks and savings accounts — so they can spend more later.

≈ Adam Davidson

In this book, I've tried to give you a substantive, unbiased perspective on managing your money wisely and achieving a fulfilling retirement. Granted, it's a topic that could fill several books, but I hope what you have read at the very least motivates you into thinking seriously about your financial future and the quality of life you hope to experience in retirement. Let me amend that: I hope what you have read takes you beyond the thinking stage and propels you into taking positive action.

As mentioned earlier, procrastination is perhaps the greatest threat to a successful retirement. It saddens me to hear stories of people who were so busy accumulating possessions they never got around to accumulating enough money to truly enjoy their later years. Planning for retirement is easily deferred if no one is there to prod you into taking control of your future. Hopefully, this book will provide you with the necessary nudge.

You cannot expect the government, your employer or anyone else to assume responsibility for your future. You must take charge yourself. It's a personal responsibility for each of us, and each day that passes by without a sound plan moves you one day closer to an unrewarding retirement.

I urge you to reread the chapters on *Behavioral*, *Financial* and *Lifestyle Obstacles* so you become acutely aware of the impediments to successful retirement planning. Once able to recognize these threats, you can more easily avoid their debilitating impact.

I believe there is great value in establishing a relationship with a trustworthy advisor. Setting aside the numerous studies illustrating how people who use an advisor tend to accumulate more wealth, just being able to tap into the empirical knowledge of an experienced financial professional is a meaningful advantage for virtually any individual. Of course, knowing what to ask in order to find an advisor best suited to meet your expectations is critical. The chapter on *Advisor Intangibles* should be a big help for you.

Finding a competent and compatible financial advisor is arguably as important as finding a competent physician. Each helps safeguard your health, whether financial or physical. In simple terms, a capable advisor can help you be better prepared for retirement. That means being able to live well, enjoy your later years, and do the things you dream of doing without fear of running out of money over the long term. That's a really big deal and I don't think dedicated financial advisors are given enough credit for how they help clients manage and protect their money through the fluctuating economic environments that occur over a lifetime. It's a huge responsibility.

In addition to helping clients manage their money, a big part of advisory relationships is helping clients avoid making mistakes. When I see retirees withdrawing too much money, it's my duty to warn them that if they keep taking out 8% or 9% on a regular basis, they're likely to run out of money. Just having someone who has seen others make that mistake can be a valuable asset to an individual or couple who may not fully comprehend withdrawal calculations.

Your advisor should be a good coach, someone to tell you how to do things better and warn you when you are about to do something wrong or get ahead of yourself. Just last week, a client who is managing money in a trust for his brother called me to say he wants to increase the amount his brother receives each month by $700. A simple calculation showed that doing so was unsustainable and that his brother would run out of money in less than a decade. It wasn't what he wanted to hear, but it was vital that he hear it. Being a trustee is a major responsibility and there are laws regarding proper trust administration. That's the value of having an advisor who has the latitude (and courage) to say "no" when necessary.

Another consideration is the constantly changing financial environment. Regulations and limits regarding CPP, TFSA, RESP and other factors are constantly changing, not to mention tax law changes. You certainly want an advisor who takes responsibility for keeping up to date on all the various issues and investment products, and makes sure you are well looked after during this time of continuous change.

Pension plans have also undergone a major transformation over the past couple of decades. Whereas pensions with guaranteed benefits were commonplace years ago, today's pensions are almost all defined contribution plans that place responsibility for investment choices and performance on the individual. Again, personal responsibility is replacing employer or governmental assurances. More and more, the responsibility for making sure you have enough money to retire on is yours and no one else's.

Healthcare is another issue that you need to think about. Aging baby boomers have created a bulge in the healthcare system that's only going to get more pronounced as they continue to age into their 70s and beyond. Quality healthcare is going to become increasingly expensive. We have a public system here in Canada but it's not without problems. I recently read about a senior here in Abbotsford, British Columbia who was told by his physician that a tumor on his throat was terminal. The man's Korean wife was unconvinced. She tried to get her husband an appointment with an oncologist at the cancer clinic but was repeatedly postponed. She finally decided to take her husband to Korea for treatment, where he had an operation followed by radiation and chemo. He is now cancer free.

The example points out to increasing stress our Canadian healthcare system is being subjected to. As people age and live longer, the backlog for specialized treatment can only grow worse. Individuals, again, will have to be responsible for having sufficient wealth to manage their healthcare with private treatment if necessary.

While this book does not have room to cover every nuance of wealth accumulation and retirement planning, there are additional resources available to you. The Internet has an almost inexhaustible supply of information regarding the topic but be wary of the source and validity of what you find.

To help our clients gain a better understanding of the issues, our firm conducts regular workshops on a broad array of related topics, including taxes (both Canadian and U.S.), retirement planning, estate planning, women's issues and other important subjects. You're welcome to contact our office: 604.451.3100, visit our website: www.muironmoney.com or email Eric.Muir@raymondjames.ca for information about our workshops.

[1] CBC News| Health, 15 May 2014.

[2] Harris/Decima poll conducted on behalf of the Canadian Imperial Bank of Commerce.

[3] Jason Fekete, Postmedia News, December 16, 2013.

[4] www.inflation.eu

[5] Reinhart Niebuhr (1872-1971).

[6] Statistics Canada

[7] Canadian Institute of Actuaries mortality table UP-94.

[8] Holmes-Rahe Life Stress Inventory, *The Social Readjustment Rating Scale.*

[9] Brad M. Barber, Graduate School of Management, University of California, Davis, CA and Terrance Odean, Haas School of Business, University of California, Berkeley, CA, "The Behavior of Individual Investors," Handbook of the Economics of Finance, 2013.

[10] Peter G. Andresen, Dollars and Common Sense (Timewalker Press, 2012) 27.

[11] Robert Stammers, Director, Investor Education, CFA Institute, "Three Behavioral Biases That Can Affect Your Investment Performance," Forbes, Dec 21, 2011.

[12] Christopher B. Philips and Francis M. Kinniry Jr., "The role of home bias in global asset allocation decisions," Vanguard research June 2012.

[13] Michael Klika and Martin Weber, "Home Bias in International Stock Return Expectations," Journal of Psychology and Financial Markets, June 2010 176-192.

[14] Beni Lauterbach and Haim Reisman, "Keeping Up with the Jonses and the Home Bias," European Financial Management, June 2004.

[15] James Jay Mooreland II, "The Irrational Investor's Risk Profile," (thesis submitted to the Graduate School of the University of Minnesota, May 2011.

[16] A cognitive bias is a pattern of deviation in judgment that occurs in particular situations. Cognitive biases are instances of evolved mental behavior. (www.princeton.edu).

[17] Larry Swedroe, "Why Investors are their own worst enemy," <u>Moneywatch</u>, March 26, 2012.

[18] www12.statcan.gc.ca/census

[19] Chris Li, Income Statistics Division, Statistics Canada, "Widowhood: Consequences on Income for Senior Women." July 2004.

[20] David Solomon, Eugene Soltes and Denis Sosyura, "Winners in the Spotlight Media Coverage of Fund Holdings as a Driver of Flows," <u>Journal of Financial Economics</u> July 2014, 53-72.

[21] Christopher Carosa, "Mass Media Retirement Hype," Fiduciary News Feb 1, 2011.

[22] Paul C. Tetlock, "Giving Content to Investor Sentiment: The Role of Media in the Stock Market," Columbia Business School – Finance and Economics 21 March 2005.

[23] Larry MacDonald, "Media's influence on stock market," <u>Canadian Business</u> 24 June 2009.

[24] Lily Fang and Joel Peress, "Media Coverage and the Cross-section of Stock Returns," <u>The Journal of Finance</u> Oct.2009 Volume 64, 2023-2052.
[25] Robert D. Arnott and Denis B. Chaves, Financial Analysts Journal, Jan/Feb 2012.

[26] Includes income from employment, business, real estate rentals, royalties, taxable support payments, CPP or provincial disability pensions, and money received from a supplementary unemployment benefit plan — excluding federal employment insurance.

[27] For RRSP purposes, earned income is the annual total of: employment income, net rental income, net income from self-employment, royalties, research grants, alimony or maintenance payments, disability payments from CPP or QPP and supplementary UIC payments.

[28] www.trialandheirs.com

[29] www.americanwillsandestates.com

[30] www.legalzoom.com

[31] Raymond James research

[32] www.nidus.ca

[33] www.investopedia.com

[34] Deemed disposition means that upon death, all your assets are deemed to have been sold at fair market value, triggering the payment of income or capital gains taxes. In addition to capital gain, property that has been depreciated is subject to a recapture of capital cost allowance.

[35] www.invesco.ca

CPSIA information can be obtained
at www.ICGtesting.com
Printed in the USA
LVOW06s2344210316

480156LV00019B/89/P